HANDBOOK OF NATURE STUDY:

WILDFLOWERS, WEEDS,
CULTIVATED CROPS

COMPLETE YOUR COLLECTION TODAY!

Handbook of
Nature-Study:
Wildflowers, Weeds and
Cultivated Crops

ANNA BOTSFORD COMSTOCK, B.S., L.H.D

LATE PROFESSOR OF NATURE-STUDY IN CORNELL UNIVERSITY

LIVING BOOK
PRESS

This edition published 2020
by Living Book Press

Copyright © Living Book Press, 2020

ISBN: 978-1-922348-60-9 (hardcover)
         978-1-922348-61-6 (softcover)

A catalogue record for this
book is available from the
National Library of Australia

CONTENTS

White mountain laurel

How to Begin the Study of Plants and Flowers

THE only right way to begin plant study with young children is through awakening their interest in and love for flowers. Most children love flowers naturally; they enjoy bringing flowers to school, and here, by teaching the recognition of flowers by name, may be begun this delightful study. This should be done naturally and informally. The teacher may say: "Thank you, John, for this bouquet. Why, here is a pansy, a bachelor's button, a larkspur and a poppy." Or, "Julia has brought me a beautiful flower. What is its name, I wonder?" Then may follow a little discussion, which the teacher leads to the proper conclusion. If this course is consistently followed, the children will learn the names of the common flowers of wood, field and garden, and never realize that they are learning anything.

The next step is to inspire the child with a desire to care for and preserve his bouquet. The posies brought in the perspiring little hand may be wilted and look dejected; ask their owner to place the stems in water and call attention to the way they lift their drooping heads. Parents and teachers should very early inculcate in children this respect for the rights of flowers which they gather; no matter how tired the child or how disinclined to further effort, when he returns from the woods or fields or garden with plucked flowers, he should be made to place their stems in water immediately. This is a lesson in duty as well as in plant study. Attention to the behavior of the thirsty flowers may be gained by asking the following questions:

1. When a plant is wilted how does it look? How does its stem act? Do its leaves stand up? What happens to the flower?

2. Place the cut end of the stem in water and look at it occasionally during an hour; describe what happens to the stem, the leaves, the blossom.

3. To find how flowers drink, place the stem of a wilted plant in red ink; the next day cut the stem across and find how far the ink has been lifted into it.

Colorado blue columbine aquilegia

How To Make Plants Comfortable

NOTHER step in plant study comes naturally from planting the seeds in window-boxes or garden. This may be done in the kindergarten or in the primary grades. As soon as the children have had some experience in the growing of flowers, they should conduct some experiments which will teach them about the needs of plants. These experiments are fit for the work of the second or third grade. Uncle John says, "All plants want to grow; all they ask is that they shall be made comfortable." The following experiments should be made vital and full of interest, by impressing upon the children that through them they will learn to make their plants comfortable.

EXPERIMENT 1. *To find out what kind of soil plants love best to grow in—* Have the children of a class, or individuals representing a class, prepare four little pots or boxes, as follows: Fill one with rich, woods humus, or with potting earth from a florist's; another with poor, hard soil, which may be found near excavations; another with clean sand; another with sawdust. Plant the same kind of seeds in all four, and place them where they will get plenty of light. Water them as often as needful. Note which plants grow the best. This trial should cover six weeks at least and attention should now and then be called to the relative growth of the plants.

EXPERIMENT 2. *To prove that plants need light in order to grow.*— Fill two pots with the same rich soil; plant in these the same kind of seeds, and give them both the same amount of water; keep one in the window and place the other in a dark closet or under a box, and note what happens. Or take two potted geraniums which look equally thrifty; keep one in the light and the other in darkness. What happens?

EXPERIMENT 3. *To show that the leaves love the light*— Place a geranium in a window and let it remain in the same position for two weeks. Which way do all the leaves face? Turn it around, and note what the leaves have done after a few days.

A terrarium. Various plants can be grown, and many kinds of insects, reptiles or amphibians can be perfectly at home in a terrarium that is suitable sized.

EXPERIMENT 4. *To show that plants need water*— Fill three pots with rich earth, plant the same kinds of seeds in each, and place them all in the same window. Give one water as it needs it, keep another flooded with water, and give the other none at all. What happens to the seeds in the three pots?

The success of these four experiments depends upon the genius of the teacher. The interest in the result should be keen; every child should feel that every seed planted is a living germ and that it is struggling to grow; every look at the experiments should be like another chapter in a continued story. In the case of young children, I have gone so far as to name the seeds, "Robbie Radish" or "Polly Peppergrass." I did this to focus the attention of the child on the efforts of this living being to grow. After the experiments, the children told the story, personating each seed, thus: "I am Susie Sweet Pea and Johnny Smith planted me in sand. I started to grow, for I had some lunch with me which my mother put up for me to eat when I was hungry; but after

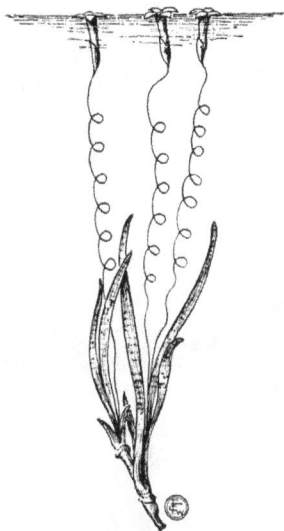

Eel grass, Vallisneria. A quiet-water plant, eel grass produces its male flowers under water, its female flowers bloom at the top. When mature, the male flowers float to the surface, where pollination occurs; the female flowers are then retracted to mature the fruits under water. This plant is the favorite food of canvasback ducks

the lunch was all gone, I could find very little food in the sand, although my little roots reached down and tried and tried to find something for me to eat. I finally grew pale and could not put out another leaf."

The explanations of these experiments should be simple, with no attempt to teach the details of plant physiology. The need of plants for rich, loose earth and for water is easily understood by the children; but the need for light is not so apparent, and Uncle John's story of the starch factory is the most simple and graphic way of making known to the children the processes of plant nourishment. This is how he tells it: "Plants are just like us; they have to have food to make them grow; where is the food and how do they find it? Every green leaf is a factory to make food for the plant; the green pulp in the leaf is the machinery; the leaves get the raw materials from the sap and from the air, and the machinery unites them and makes them into plant food. This is mostly starch, for this is the chief food of plants, although they require some other kinds of food also. The machinery is run by sunshine-power, so the leaf-factory can make nothing without the aid of light; the leaf-factories begin to work as soon as the sun rises, and only stop working when it sets. But the starch has to be changed to sugar before the baby, growing tips of the plant can use it for nourishment and growth; and so the leaves, after making the starch from the sap and the air, are obliged to digest it, changing the starch to sugar; for the growing parts of the plant feed upon sweet sap. Although the starch-factory in the leaves can work only during the daytime, the leaves can change the starch to sugar during the night. So far as we know, there is no starch in the whole world which is not made in the leaf-factories."

Birch trees. Although these birches grow in clumps, several trunks from a common root, observe that the trunks soon separate widely, thus providing abundant light for the leaves

This story should be told and repeated often, until the children realize the work done by leaves for the plants and their need of light.

> *"The clouds are at play in the azure space*
> *And their shadows at play on the bright green vale.*
> *And here they stretch to the frolic chase;*
> *And there they roll on the easy gale.*
> *"There's a dance of leaves in that aspen bower,*
> *There's a titter of winds in that beechen tree,*
> *There's a smile on the fruit and a smile on the flower,*
> *And a laugh from the brook that runs to the sea."*
>
> —BRYANT.

How To Teach the Names of the Parts of a Flower and of the Plant

HE scientific names given to the parts of plants have been the stumbling block to many teachers, and yet no part of plant study is more easily accomplished. First of all, the teacher should have in mind clearly the names of the parts which she wishes to teach; the illustrations here given are for her convenience. When talking with the pupils about flowers let her use these names naturally:

"See how many geraniums we have; the corolla of this one is red and of that one is pink. The red corolla has fourteen petals and the pink one only five," etc.

"This arbutus which James brought has a pretty little pink bell for a corolla."

"The purple trillium has a purple corolla, the white trillium a white corolla; and both have green sepals."

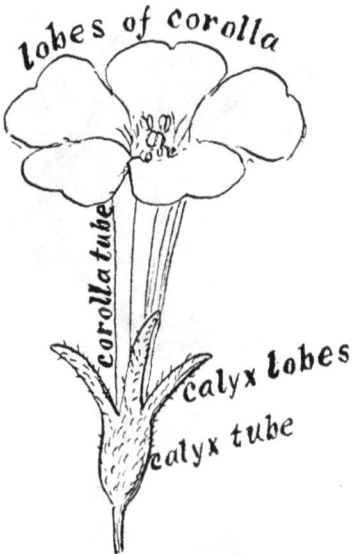

A flower with petals united forming a tube, and with sepals likewise united.

The points to be borne in mind are that children like to call things by their names because they are *real* names, and they also like to use "grown up" names for things; but they do not like to commit to memory names which to them are meaningless. Circumlocution is a waste of breath; calling a petal a "leaf of a flower" or the petiole "the stem of a leaf," is like calling a boy's arm "the projecting part of James' body" or Molly's golden hair "the yellow top" to her head. All the names should be taught gradually by constant unemphasized use on

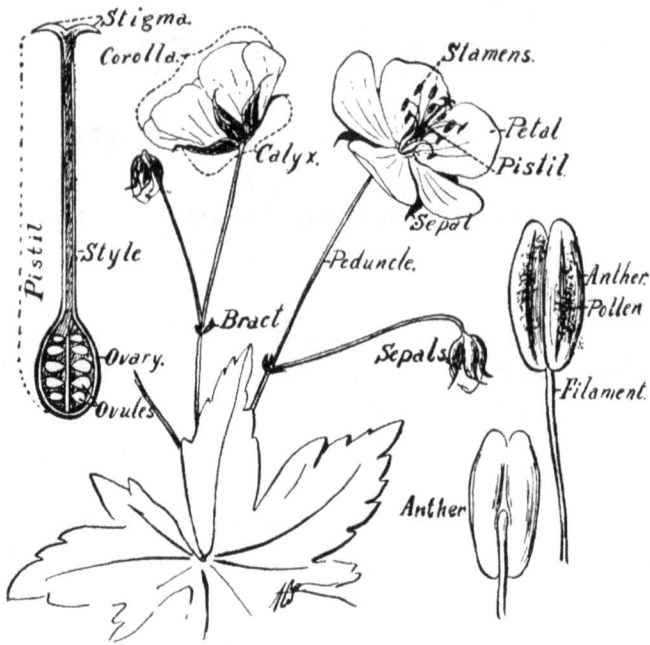

A flower with the parts named

the part of the teacher; and if the child does not learn the names naturally then do not make him do it unnaturally.

The lesson on the garden, or horseshoe geranium with single flowers, is the one to be given first in teaching the structure of a flower since the geranium blossom is simple and easily understood.

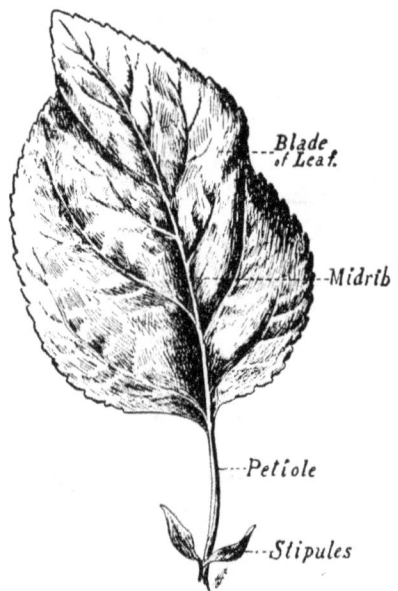

A leaf with parts named.

Pomegranate fruit

Teach the Use of the Flower

FROM first to last the children should be taught that the object of the flower is to develop seed. They should look eagerly into the maturing flower for the growing fruit. Poetry is full of the sadness of the fading flower, while rightly it should be the gladness of the flower that fades, because its work is done for the precious seed at its heart. The whole attention of the child should be fixed upon the developing fruit instead of the fading and falling petals.

"In all places then and in all seasons,
Flowers expand their light and soul-like wings,
Teaching us by most persuasive reasons,
How akin they are to human things."

—LONGFELLOW.

Honey bee collecting pollen from a flower. The bee can carry pollen from one flower to another

Flowers and Insect Partners

T is undoubtedly true that while the processes of cross-pollenation and the complicated devices of flowers for insuring it can only be well taught to older pupils and only fully understood in the college laboratory, yet there are a few simple facts which even the young child may know, as follows:

1. Pollen is needed to make the seeds grow; some flowers need the pollen from other flowers of the same kind, to make their seeds grow; but many flowers also use the pollen from their own flowers to pollenate their ovules, which grow into seeds.

2. Flowers have neither legs like animals nor wings like butterflies, to go after pollen; so they give insects nectar to drink and pollen to eat, and thus pay them for fetching and carrying the pollen.

I taught this to a four-year-old once in the following manner: A pine tree in the yard was sifting its pollen over us and little Jack asked what the yellow dust was; we went to the tree and saw where it came from, then I found a tiny young cone and explained to him that this was a pine blos-

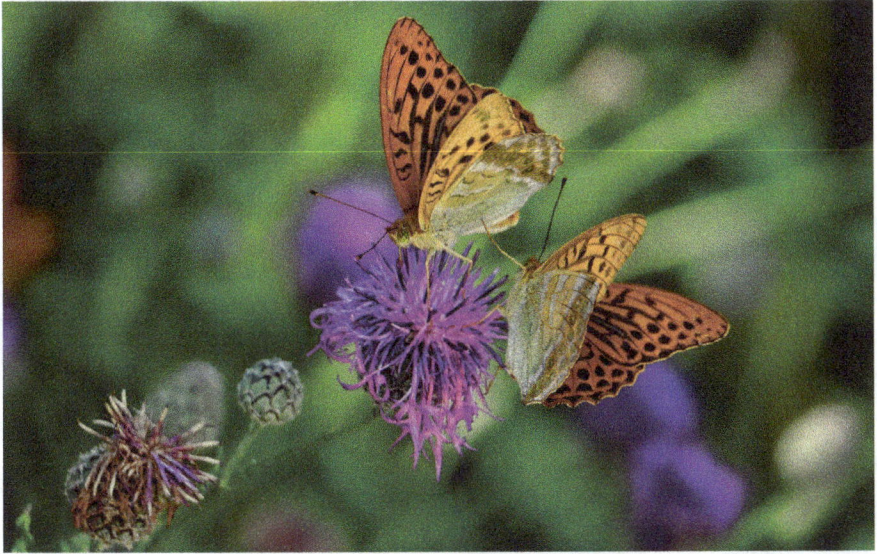

Butterflies are also great pollinators

som, and that in order to become a cone with seeds, it must have some pollen fall upon it; and we saw how the wind sifted the pollen over it and then we examined a ripe cone and found the seeds. Then we looked at the clovers in the lawn. They did not have so much pollen and they were so low in the grass that the wind could not carry it for them; but right there was a bee. What was she doing? She was getting honey for her hive or pollen for her brood, and she went from one clover head to another; we caught her in a glass fruit jar, and found she was dusted with pollen and that she had pollen packed in the baskets on her hind legs; and we concluded that she carried plenty of pollen on her clothes for the clovers, and that the pollen in her baskets was for her own use. After that he was always watching the bees at work; and we found afterwards that flowers had two ways of telling the insects that they wanted pollen. One was by their color, for the dandelions and clovers hide their colors during dark, rainy days when the bees remain in their hives. Then we found the bees working on mignonette, whose blossoms were so small that Jack did not think they were blossoms at all, and we concluded that the mignonette called the bees by its fragrance. We found other flowers which called with both color and fragrance; and this insect-flower partnership remained a factor of great interest in the child's mind ever after.

Pollen on a bees leg as it visits flowers

"Roly-poly honey-bee,
Humming in the clover,
Under you the tossing leaves,
And the blue sky over,
Why are you so busy, pray?
Never still a minute,
Hovering now above a flower,
Now half buried in it!"

—Julia C. R. Dorr.

The Relation of Plants to Geography

THERE should be from first to last a steady growth in the intelligence of the child as to the places where certain plants grow. He finds hepaticas and trilliums in the woods, daisies and buttercups in the sunny fields, mullein on the dry hillsides, cat-tails in the swamp, and water lilies floating on the pond. This may all be taught by simply asking the pupils questions relating to the soil and the special conditions of the locality where they found the flowers they bring to school.

The plants found in a mountain forest (top) and a rainforest (above) are very different

Newly germinated plants. See the seed shell still stuck to the tips of the original leaves

Seed Germination

Less than three decades ago, this one feature of plant life once came near "gobbling up" all of nature-study, and yet it is merely an incident in the growth of the plant. To sprout seeds is absurd as an object in itself; it is incidental as is the breaking of the egg-shell to the study of the chicken. The peeping into a seed like a bean or a pea, to see that the plant is really there, with its lunch put up by its mother packed all around it, is interesting to the child. To watch the little plant develop, to study its seed-leaves and what becomes of them, to know that they give the plant its first food and to know how a young plant looks and acts, are all items of legitimate interest in the study of the life of a plant; in fact the struggle of the little plant to get free from its seed-coats may be a truly dramatic story. (See "First Lessons with Plants," Bailey, page 79). But to regard this feature as the chief object of planting seed is manifestly absurd.

The object of planting any seed should be to rear a plant which shall fulfill its whole duty and produce other seed. The following observations regarding the germination of seeds should be made while the children are eagerly watching the coming of the plants in their gardens or window-boxes:

1. Which comes out of the seed first, the root or the leaf? Which way does the root always grow, up or down? Which way do the leaves always grow, no matter which side up the seed is planted?

Seeds can be germinated almost anywhere. Here an egg carton has been used

2. How do the seed-leaves try to get out of the seed-coat, or shell? How do the seed-leaves differ in form from the leaves which come later? What becomes of the seed-leaves after the plant begins to grow?

References— First Lessons with Plants, L. H. Bailey; First Lessons in Plant Life, Atkinson; Plants and their Children, Dana; Plants, Coulter; How Plants Grow, Gray; How Plants Behave, Gray.

A hazelnut seedling

WILDFLOWERS

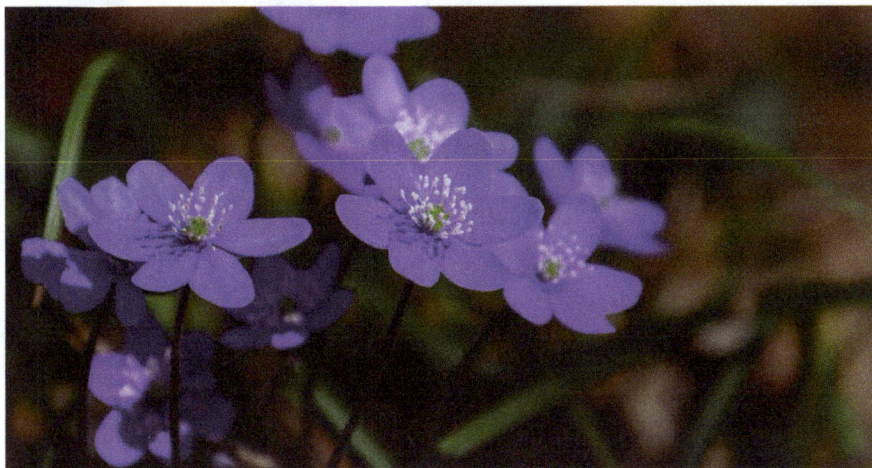
Hepaticas in their natural surrounding

The Hepatica

TEACHER'S STORY

"The wise men say the hepatica flower has no petals but has pink, white or purple sepals instead: and they say, too, that the three leaflets of the cup which holds the flower are not sepals but are bracts; and they offer as proof the fact that they do not grow close to the blossom, but are placed a little way down the stem. But the hepatica does not care what names the wise men give to the parts of its blossom: it says as plainly as if it could talk: 'The bees do not care whether they are sepals or petals since they are pretty in color, and show where the pollen is to be found. I will teach the world that bracts are just as good to wrap around flower-buds as are sepals, and that sepals may be just as beautiful as petals. Since my petticoat is pretty enough for a dress why should not I wear it thus?'"

—"THE CHILD'S OWN BOOK OF WILD FLOWERS."

We seek the hepatica in its own haunts, because there is a longing for spring in our hearts that awakens with the first warm sunshine. As we thread our way into sodden woods, avoiding the streams and puddles which are little glacial rivers and lakes, having their sources in the snow-drifts still heaped on the north side of things, we look

Hepatica

eagerly for signs of returning life. Our eyes slowly distinguish among the various shades of brown in the floor of the forest, a bit of pale-blue or pink-purple that at first seems like an optical delusion; but as we look again to make sure, Lo! it is the hepatica, lifting its delicate blossoms above its mass of purple-brown leaves. These leaves, moreover, are always beautiful in shape and color and suggest patterns for sculpture like the acanthus, or for rich tapestries like the palm-leaf in the Orient. It warms the heart to see these brave little flowers stand with their faces to the sun and their backs to the snow-drifts, looking out on a gray-brown world, nodding to it and calling it good.

The hepatica is forehanded in several ways. After the leaves have fallen from the trees in the autumn and let in the sunshine, it puts up new leaves which make food that is stored in the crown bud; the little flower buds are then started, and wrapped cozily, are cuddled down at the very center of the plant. These buds, perfected in the autumn, are ready to stretch up and blossom when the first warmth of spring shall reach them. The stems and the bracts of the flower are soft and downy, and are much more furry than those which appear later; while this down is not for the purpose of keeping the plant at a higher temperature, yet it acts as a blanket to prevent too rapid transpiration, which is a cooling process, and thus it does, as a matter of fact, keep the flower warmer. As the stems lift up, the buds are bent, which position protects them from the beating storms. The hepatica flowers are white, pink and lavender. The latter are sometimes called "blue." The so-called "petals" number from six to twelve; there are usually six. The three outer ones are sepals and are exactly like the three inner ones, the petals, but may be distinguished by their outside position in the half-opened flower. The three green bracts which encase the flower bud, and later remain with the seed, are placed on the stem quite distinctly below the flower. On dark days and during the nights, the young blossoms close; but when they become old and faded, they remain open all the time. Thus, the flowers are closed except when bees are likely to visit them; but after they have shed their pollen, they do not need to remain closed any longer. Not all hepatica blossoms are fragrant; and those that are so, lose their fragrance as their colors begin to fade to white. If a snow-storm comes, the hepatica blossoms close and bow their heads.

There are many stamens with greenish white anthers and pollen. They stand erect around the many pistils at the center of the flower. The number of pistils varies from six to twenty-four. Each pistil holds aloft the little horseshoe-shaped, whitish stigma and, if pollenated, develops into a seed. The hepatica is a perennial and grows only in rich, moist woods. It is so adapted to the shade, that it dies if transplanted to sunny places. The leaves which have passed the winter under the snow are rich purple beneath, and mottled green and purple above, making beautiful objects for water-color drawings. The new leaves are put forth in spring before the leaves of the trees create too much shade. In the fall, after the trees are bare, the leaves again become active. The roots are quite numerous and fine.

Embroidery design from the hepatica

LESSON

Leading thought— The hepatica flower buds are developed in the fall, so as to be ready to blossom early in the spring. This plant lives only in moist and shady woods.

Method— The pupils should have the questions before they go into the woods to gather spring flowers, and should answer them individually. However, the hepatica plant may be potted early in the spring, and the flowers may be watched during their development, and studied in the schoolroom.

Observations—

1. Where do you find the hepaticas? Do you ever find them in the open fields? Do you ever find them in the pine woods?

2. How do the leaves look in early spring? Sketch in color one of these old leaves. How do the young leaves look? Are the leaves that come up late in the spring as fuzzy as those that appear early? What is the difference in texture and color between the leaves that were perfected in the fall and those that appear in the spring?

3. Find a hepatica plant before it begins to blossom. Look, if possible, at its very center. Describe these little flower buds. When were they formed?

4. How does the bud look when it begins to lift up? Describe the stems and the three little blankets that hold the bud. Ask your teacher how these fuzzy blankets keep the bud from being killed by cold.

5. Are the hepaticas in your woods all pink, or blue, or white? Do those which are at first pink or blue fade to white later? Do the blossoms keep open during the night and stormy weather? Why not? Are they all fragrant?

Hepatica growing in the wild

6. How many petals has your hepatica? Can you see that the outer ones are sepals, although they look just like the petals? Peel back the three sepal-like bracts and see that they are not a part of the flower at all but join the stem below the flower.

7. Describe the stamens in the hepatica. How many pistils are there? Does each pistil develop into a seed? How do the three bracts protect the seeds as they ripen?

8. What insects do you find visiting the hepaticas?

9. Describe a hepatica plant in the woods; mark it so that you will know it, and visit it occasionally during the summer and autumn, noting what happens to it.

Yellow Adder's Tongue or Dog's Tooth Violet

The Yellow Adder's Tongue

"Once a prize was offered to a child if she would find two leaves of the adder's tongue that were marked exactly alike: and she sought long and faithfully, but the only prize she won was a lesson in Nature's book of variations, where no two leaves of any plant, shrub or tree are exactly alike: for even if they seemed so to our eyes, yet there would exist in them differences of strength and growth too subtle for us to detect. But this child was slow in learning this great fact, and, until she was a woman, the adder's tongue leaves, so beautifully embroidered with purple and green, were to her a miracle, revealing the infinite diversity of Nature's patterns."

—"The Child's Own Book of Wild Flowers."

This little lily of the woods is a fascinating plant. Its leaves of pale green mottled with brownish purple often cover closely large irregular areas in the rich soil of our woodlands; and yet I doubt if the under-

Dog's Tooth Violets in natural surrounding

ground story of these forest rugs is often thought of. The leaves are twins, and to the one who plucks them carelessly they seem to come from one slender stem. It requires muscle as well as decision of character to follow this weak stem down several inches, by digging around it, until we find the corm at its base. A corm is the swollen base of a stem and is bulb-like in form; but it is not made up of layers, as is a bulb. It is a storehouse for food and also a means of spreading the species; for from the corms there grow little corms called cormels, and each cormel develops a separate plant. This underground method of reproduction is the secret of why the leaves of the adder's tongue appear in patches, closely crowded together.

Only a few of the plants in a "patch" produce flowers, and it is interesting to see how cleverly these lily bells hide from the casual eye. Like many of the lilies, the three sepals are petal-like and are identified as sepals only by their outside position, although they are thicker in texture. They are purplish brown outside, which serves to render the flower inconspicuous as we look down upon it; on the inner side, they are a pure yellow, spotted with darker yellow near where they join the stem. The three petals are pure yellow, paler outside than in, and they

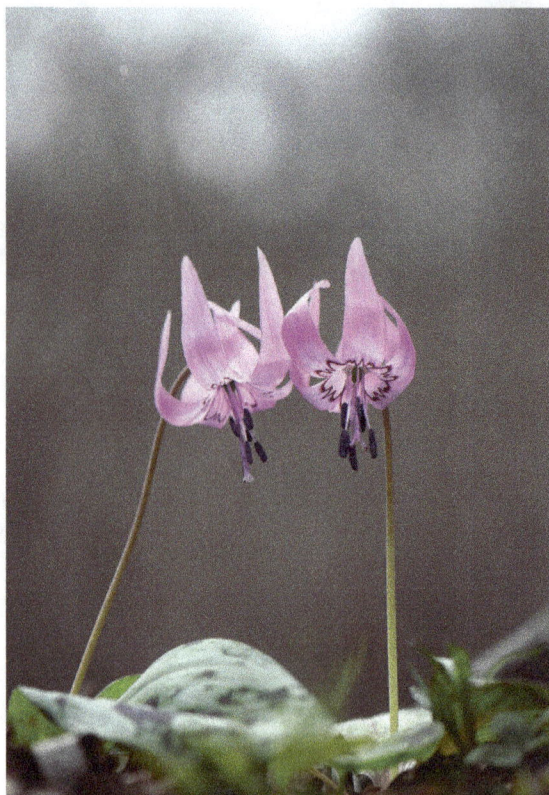

have dark spots like the tiger lilies near the heart of the flower; and where they join the stem, each has on each side an ear-shaped lobe.

The open flower is bell-shaped; and like other bells it has a clapper, or tongue. This is formed by six downward-hanging stamens, the yellow filaments of which have broad bases and taper to points where the oblong anthers join them. The anthers are red or yellow. It is this stamen clapper that the visiting insects must cling to when probing upward for nectar from this flower at the upper end of the bell. The pale green pistil is somewhat three-sided, and the long style remains attached long after the flower disappears.

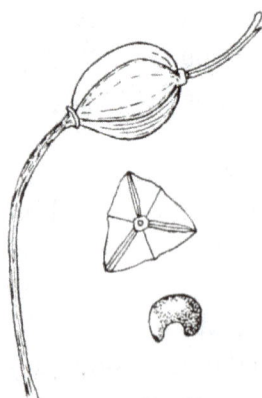

Fruit capsule and seed

The flower is slightly fragrant, and it is visited by the queen bumblebees and the solitary bees, of which there are many species. The flower closes nights and during cloudy, stormy days. The seed capsule is plump and rather triangular, and splits into three sections when ripe. The seeds are numerous and are fleshy and crescent-shaped.

But the adder's tongue, like many other early blooming flowers, is a child of the spring. The leaves, at first so prettily mottled, fade out to plain green; and by midsummer they have entirely disappeared, the place where they

26

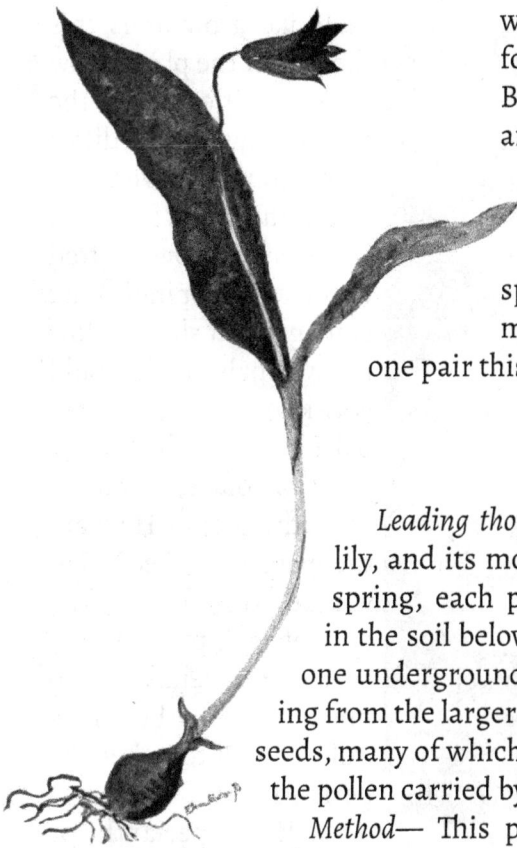

were, being covered with other foliage of far different pattern. But down in the rich woods soil are the plump globular corms filled with the food gathered by the spotted leaves during their brief stay, and next spring two pairs of spotted leaves may appear where there was but one pair this year.

LESSON

Leading thought— The adder's tongue is a lily, and its mottled leaves appear early in the spring, each pair coming from a corm deep in the soil below. It has two ways of spreading, one underground by means of new corms growing from the larger ones, and the other by means of seeds, many of which are probably perfected through the pollen carried by insects.

Method— This plant should be studied in the woods, notes being made on it there. But a plant showing corm, roots, leaves and blossom should be brought to the schoolhouse for detailed study, and then planted in a shady place in the school garden.

Observations—

1. Where does the adder's tongue grow? Do you ever find it in open fields? How early do you find its leaves above ground? At what time do its blossoms appear?

2. How many leaves has each plant? What colors do you find in them? What is the color of their petioles? Do the leaves remain mottled later in the season?

3. Do the adder's tongue plants occur singly or in patches? Dig out a plant and see if you can find why the plants grow so many together?

4. How far below the surface of the ground did you find the corm or

Dog's Tooth Violet ready to flower

bulb-like growth? Is this the root of the plant? How does it differ from the roots? How does it differ from a bulb? Of what use is it to the plant?

5. Is the flower lifted up, or is it drooping? What is its general shape? How many sepals? How would you know they were sepals? How do they differ in color, outside and in, from the petals? How are the petals marked? Can you see the lobes at the base of each petal? When sepals and petals are so much alike the botanists call them all together the perianth.

6. If the perianth, or the sepals and petals together, make a bell-shaped flower, what makes the clapper to the bell? How do the insects use this clapper when they visit the flower? Do the flowers stay open nights and dark days? Why?

7. How many stamens are there? Describe or sketch one, noting its peculiar shape. Are the stamens all the same length? Can you see the pistil and its stigma? Where is it situated in relation to the stamens? Do you think the stigma is ready for pollen at the time the anthers are shedding it?

8. After the petals and sepals fall what remains? How does the ripe seed-capsule look? How does it open to let out the seeds? Are there many seeds in a capsule? What is their shape?

Bloodroot

TEACHER'S STORY

"What time the earliest ferns unfold,
And meadow cowslips count their gold;
A countless multitude they stood,
A Milky Way within the wood."

—DANSKE DANDRIDGE.

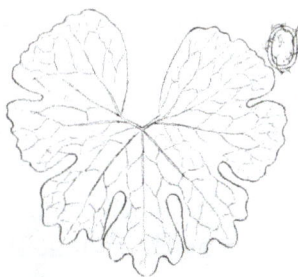

ONLY a few generations ago, and this land of ours was peopled by those who found it fitting to paint their bodies to represent their mental or spiritual conditions or intentions. For this purpose they had studied the plants of our forests to learn the secrets of the dyes which they yielded, and a dye that would remain on the flesh permanently, or until it wore off, was highly prized. Such a dye was found in the bloodroot, a dye appropriate in its color to represent a thirst for blood; and with it they made their war paint, and with it they ornamented their tomahawks to symbolize their sanguinary purpose.

The Indian warriors have passed away from our forests, and the forests themselves are passing away, but the bloodroot still lingers, growing abundantly in rich moist woods or in shaded areas in glades, borders of meadows and fence corners. Its beautiful white flowers open to the morning sun in early April, calling the hungry bees to come for pollen; for, like many other early flowers, it offers no nectar. Probably many of the little wild bees prefer pollen to nectar at this time of year, for it is an important element in the food of all kinds of bee brood. But the bloodroot's fragile blossoms are elusive and do not remain long; like their relatives, the poppies, their petals soon fall, and their white masses disappear like the snow-drifts which so recently occupied the same nooks.

The way the bloodroot leaf enfolds the flower-bud seems like such an obvious plan for protection, that we are unthinkingly prone to attribute consciousness to the little plants.

Not only does the leaf enfold the bud, but it continues to enfold the flower stem after the blossom opens. There are two sepals which enclose the bud, but fall off as the flower opens. There are ordinarily eight white petals, although there may be twelve; usually every other one of the eight petals is longer than its neighbors, and this makes the blossom rather square than circular in outline. There are many stamens, often 24, and the anthers are brilliant yellow with whitish filaments. The two-lobed stigma opens to receive pollen before the pollen of its own flower is ripe. The stigma is large, yellow, and set directly on the ovary, and is quite noticeable in the freshly opened blossoms. It is likely to shrivel before its home-grown pollen is ripe. The blossoms open wide on sunny mornings; the petals rise up in the afternoon and close at night, and also remain closed during dark, stormy days until they are quite old, when they remain carelessly open; they are now ready to fall to the ground at the slightest jar, leaving the oblong, green seed-pod set on the stem at a neat bevel, and perhaps still crowned with the yellowish stigma. The seed-pod is oblong and pointed and remains below the protecting leaf.

Bloodroot growing in the wild

There are many yellowish or brownish seeds.

When the plant appears above ground, the leaf is wrapped in a cylinder about the bud, and it is a very pretty leaf, especially the "wrong side," which forms the outside of the roll; it is pale green with a network of pinkish veins, and its edges are attractively lobed; the petiole is fleshy, stout and reddish amber in color. The flower stem is likewise fleshy and is tinged with raw sienna; the stems of both leaf and flower stand side by side, and are held together at the base by two scapes with parallel veins. Later in the season, the leaf having done its full duty as a nurse waxes opulent, often measuring six inches across and having a petiole ten inches long. It is then one of the most beautiful leaves in the forest carpet, its circular form and deeply lobed edges rendering it a fit subject for decorative design.

The rootstock is large and fleshy, and in it is stored the food which enables the flower to blossom early, before any food has been made by the new leaves. There are many stout and rather short roots that fringe the rootstock. Once in clearing a path through a woodland, we

The rootstock gives the bloodroot both its name and energy to grow

happened to hack off a mass of these rootstocks, and we stood aghast at the gory results. We had admired the bloodroot flowers in this place in the spring, and we felt as guilty as if we had inadvertently hacked into a friend.

LESSON

Leading thought— The bloodroot has a fleshy rootstock, in which is stored food for the nourishment of the blossom in early spring. The flower bud is at first protected by the folded leaf. The juice of the rootstock is a vivid light crimson, and was used by Indians as a war paint. The juice is acrid, and the bloodroot is not relished as food by grazing animals, but it is used by us as a medicine.

Method— The bloodroot may, in the fall, be transplanted in a pot of woods earth, care being taken not to disturb its roots. It should be placed out of doors in a protected place where it may have natural conditions, and be brought to the schoolroom for study in March, so that the whole act of the unfolding of leaves and flowers may be observed by the pupils. Otherwise the questions must be given the pupils to answer as they find the plants blossoming in the woods in April. The blossoms are too fragile to be successfully transported for study at home or school.

Observations—

1. At what time of year does bloodroot blossom? In what situations does it thrive?

2. What do we see first when the bloodroot puts its head above the soil? Where is the flower bud? How is it protected by the leaf? How does the leaf hold the flower stem after the flower is in blossom?

3. Study the flower. How many sepals has it? What is their color? What is the position of the sepals when the flower is in bud? What is their position when the flower opens? How many petals? What is their color and texture? Describe the position of the petals in the bud and in the open flower. Look straight into the flower; is its shape circular or square?

Notice the leaves still clasping around the stem

4. Do the flowers close nights and during dark days? Do the flowers longest open do this? Describe how the petals and sepals fall.

5. Describe the stamens. What is the color of the anthers? Of the pollen? Describe the pistil. Does the two-grooved stigma open before the pollen is shed, or after? What insects do you find visiting the bloodroot?

6. Sketch or describe a bloodroot leaf as it is wrapped around the stem of the flower. How are both flower stem and leaf petiole protected at the base? Describe or sketch a leaf after it is unfolded and open. Describe the difference between the upper and lower surfaces of the leaf. What sort of petiole has it? Break the petiole; what sort of juice comes from it? Describe and measure the leaf later in the season; do they all have the same number of lobes?

7. Break a bit off the root of the plant and note the color of the juice.

8. Compare the bloodroot with the poppies; do you find any resemblance in habits?

The white trillium

The Trillium

It would be well for the designer of tapestries to study the carpets of our forests for his patterns, for he would find there a new carpet every month, quite different in plan and design from the one spread there earlier or later. One of the most beautiful designs from Nature's looms is a trillium carpet, which is at its best when the white trilliums are in blossom. It is a fine study of the artistic possibilities of the triangle when reduced to terms of leaves, petals and sepals.

The trillium season is a long one; it begins in April with the purple wake-robin or birthroot, the species with purple, red, or sometimes yellowish flowers. The season ends in June with the last of the great white trilliums, which flush pink instead of fading, when old age comes upon them.

The color of the trillium flower depends upon the species studied; there are three petals, and the white and painted trilliums have the edges of the petals ruffled; the red and nodding trilliums have petals

A group of trillium

and sepals nearly the same size, but in the white trillium the sepals are narrower and shorter than the petals. The sepals are alternate with the petals, so that when we look straight into the flower we see it as a six-pointed star, three of the points being green sepals. The pistil of the trillium is six-lobed. It is dark red in the purple trillium and very large; in the white species, it is pale green and smaller; it opens at the top with three flaring stigmas. There are six stamens with long anthers, and they stand between the lobes of the pistil. The flower stalk rises from the center where three large leaves join. The flower stalk has a tendency to bend a little, and is rather delicate. The three leaves have an interesting venation, and make a good subject for careful drawing. The flower stem varies with different species, and so does the length of the stem of the plant, the latter being fleshy and green toward the top and reddish toward the root. The trilliums have a thick, fleshy, and much scarred rootstock from which extend rootlets which are often corrugated. The trilliums are perennial, and grow mostly in damp, rich woods. The painted trillium is found in cold, damp woods along the banks of brooks; the white trillium is likely to be found in large numbers in the same locality, while the purple trillium is found only

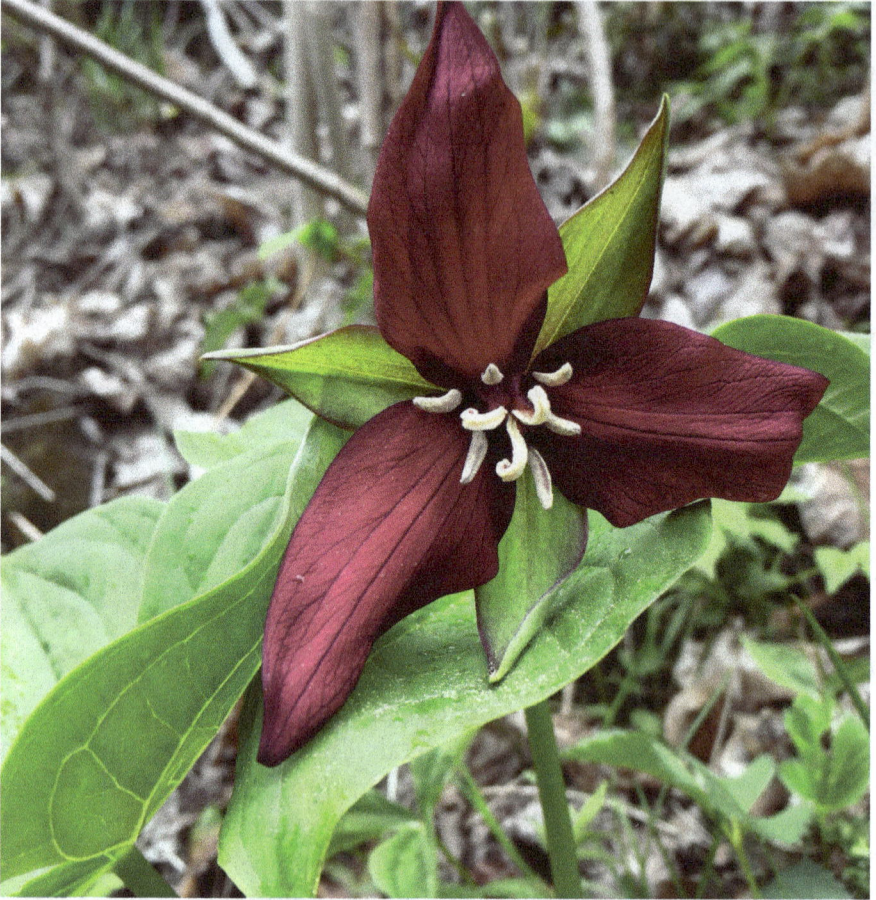

Notice the three pedals, three leaves and the three sepals.

here and there. Flies and beetles carry the pollen for the red trillium, being attracted to it by its rank odor, which is very disagreeable to us but very agreeable to them. The large white trillium is visited by bees and butterflies. The fruit of the trillium is a berry, that of the purple species is somewhat six-lobed and reddish. In late July the fruit of the white trillium is a cone with six sharp wings, or ridges, from apex to base, the latter being three-quarters of an inch across. These vertical ridges are not evenly spaced, and beneath them are packed as closely as possible the yellow-green seeds, which are as large as homeopathic pills. In cross section, it can be seen that the trillium berry is star-shaped with three compartments, the seeds growing on the partitions. This trillium fruit is very rough outside, but smooth inside, and the dried stamens often still cling to it.

The trilliums are so called from the word *triplum*, meaning three, as there are three leaves, three petals, and three sepals.

LESSON

Leading thought— The trilliums are lilies, and are often called wood lilies, because of their favorite haunts. There are several species, but they are all alike in that they have three sepals, three petals and three leaves.

Method— This lesson may be given from trilliums brought to the schoolroom by the pupils, who should be encouraged to watch the development of the berry and also to learn all the different species common to a locality.

Observations—

1. How many leaves has the trillium? How are they arranged? Draw a leaf showing its shape and veins. Describe the stem of the plant below the leaves, giving the length and color.

2. How far above the leaves does the flower stem or pedicel extend? Does the flower stand upright or droop? Describe or sketch the colors, shape and arrangement of the petals and sepals. Do the petals have ruffled margins?

3. Describe the pistil and the stigmas. Describe the stamens and how they are placed in relation to the pistil.

4. Do the flowers remain open during cloudy days and nights?

5. What insects do you find visiting the trilliums? Do the same insects visit the purple and the white trilliums? What is the difference in odor between the purple and the white trillium? Would this bring different kinds of insects to each?

6. How does the color of the white trillium change as the blossom matures? What is the color and shape of the fruit of each different species of trillium? When is the fruit ripe?

7. What kind of a root have the wake-robins? Do they grow from seed each year, or are they perennial? Where do you find them growing?

Dutchman's Breeches and Squirrel Corn

TEACHER'S STORY

"In a gymnasium where things grow,
Jolly boys and girls in a row,
Hanging down from cross-bar stem
Builded purposely for them.
Stout little legs up in the air,
Kick at the breeze as it passes there;
Dizzy heads in collars wide
Look at the world from the underside;
Happy acrobats a-swing,
At the woodside show in early spring."

A. B. C.

"And toward the sun, which kindlier burns,
The earth awaking, looks and yearns,
And still, as in all other Aprils,
The annual miracle returns."

ELIZABETH AKERS.

38

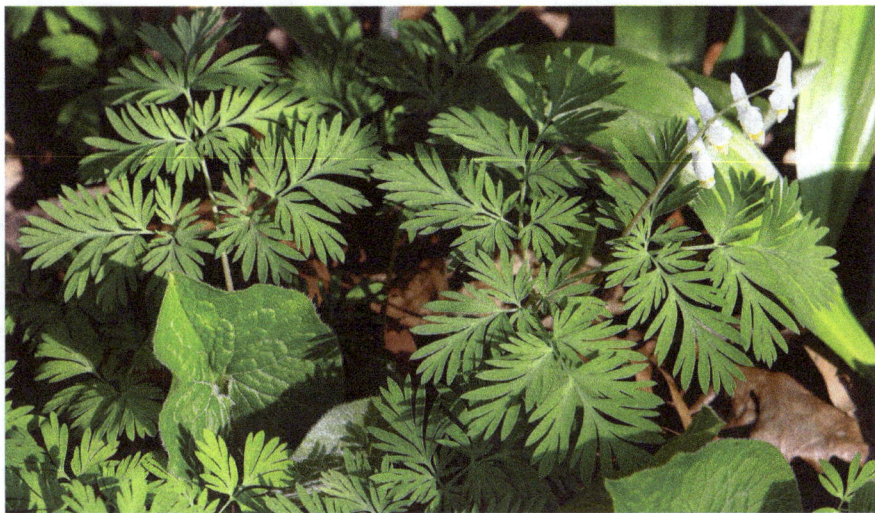

Dutchman's breeches in a garden

There are many beautiful carpets spread before the feet of advancing spring, but perhaps none of them are so delicate in pattern as those woven by these two plants that spread their fernlike leaves in April and May. There is little difference in the foliage of the two; both are delicate green and lacelike above, and pale, bluish green on the underside. And each leaf, although so finely divided, is, after all, quite simple; for it has three chief divisions, and these in turn are divided into three, and all the leaves come directly from the root and not from stems. These plants love the woodlands, and by spreading their green leaves early, before the trees are in foliage, they have the advantage of the spring sunshine. Thus they make their food for maturing their seeds, and also store some of it in their roots for use early the following spring. By midsummer the leaves have entirely disappeared, and another carpet is spread in the place which they once covered.

Dutchman's breeches and squirrel corn resemble each other so closely that they are often confused; however, they are quite different in form; the "legs" of the Dutchman's breeches are quite long and spread wide apart, while the blossoms of the squirrel corn are rounded bags instead of "legs." The roots of the two are quite different. The Dutchman's breeches grows from a little bulb made up of grayish scales, while the squirrel corn develops from a round, yellow tuber;

Squirrel Corn - *Dicentra canadensis*

Notice the underground storehouse amongst the roots of squirrel corn

these yellow, kernel-like tubers are scattered along the roots, each capable of developing a plant next year. The Dutchman's breeches likes thin woodlands and rocky hillsides, but the squirrel corn prefers rich, moist woods. The blossom of the Dutchman's breeches comes the earlier of the two. These flowers are white with yellow tips, and are not fragrant. The flowers of the squirrel corn are grayish with a tinge of magenta, and are fragrant.

The legs of the Dutchman's breeches are nectar pockets with tubes leading to them, and are formed by two petals. Opposite these two petals are two others more or less spoon-shaped, with the spoon bowls united to protect the anthers and stigma. There are two little sepals which are scalelike.

The seed capsule of the Dutchman's breeches is a long pod with a slender, pointed end, and it opens lengthwise. The seed capsules of the squirrel corn are similar and I have found in one capsule, 12 seeds, which were shaped like little kernels of corn, black in color and polished like patent leather.

LESSON

Leading thought— The Dutchman's breeches, or "boys and girls," as it is often called, is one of the earliest flowers of rich woodlands. There are interesting differences between this flower and its close relative, squirrel corn. The flowers of both of these resemble in structure the flowers of the bleeding heart.

40

Method— As the Dutchman's breeches blossoms in April and May and the squirrel corn in May and June, we naturally study the former first and compare the latter with it in form and in habits. The questions should be given the pupils, for them to answer for themselves during their spring walks in the woodlands.

Observations—

1. Where do you find Dutchman's breeches? Which do you prefer to call these flowers, Dutchman's breeches or boys and girls? Are there leaves on the trees when these flowers are in bloom?

2. Which blossoms earlier in the season, Dutchman's breeches or squirrel corn? How do the flowers of the two differ in shape? In odor?

3. In the flower of the Dutchman's breeches find two petals which protect the nectar. How do they look? What part do they form of the breeches? Find two other petals which protect the pollen and stigma.

4. Find the two sepals. How many bracts do you find on the flower stem?

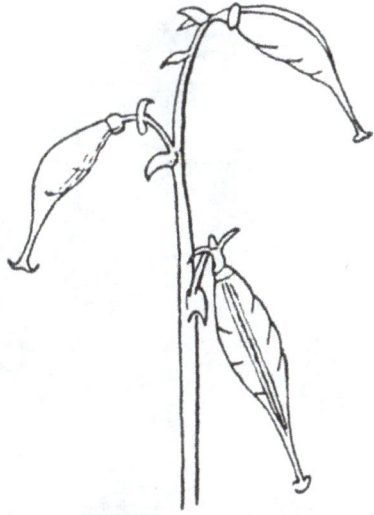
The seed capsule of squirrel corn

Dutchman's breeches closeup

Dutchman's breeches growing in the wild

5. What insects visit these flowers? Describe how they get the nectar.

6. What sort of root has the Dutchman's breeches? What is the difference between its root and that of the squirrel corn? Have you ever seen squirrels harvesting squirrel corn? What is the purpose of the kernels of the squirrel corn?

7. Study the leaf. How many main parts are there to it? How are these parts divided? Does the leaf come straight from the root or from a stem? What is the color of the leaf above? Below? Can you distinguish the leaves of the Dutchman's breeches from those of the squirrel corn?

8. Describe the seed capsule of Dutchman's breeches. How does it open? How many seeds has it? Compare this with the fruit of squirrel corn and describe the difference.

9. What happens to the leaves of these two plants late in summer? How do the plants manage to get enough sunlight to make food to mature their seed? What preparations have they made for early blossoming the next spring?

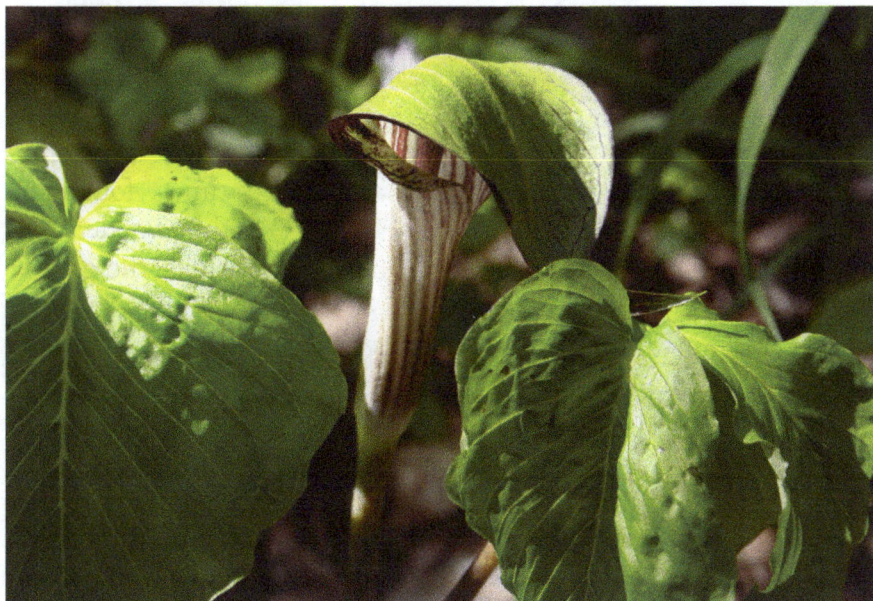

Jack-in-the-Pulpit

"With hooded heads and shields of green,
Monks of the wooded glen,
I know you well; you are, I ween,
Robin Hood's merry men."

—"CHILD'S OWN BOOK OF FLOWERS."

THIS little preacher is a prime favorite with all children, its very shape, like that of the pitcher plant, suggesting mystery; and what child could fail to lift the striped hood to discover what might be hidden beneath! And the interest is enhanced when it is discovered that the hood is but a protection for the true flowers, standing upon a club-shaped stem, which has been made through imagination into "Jack," the little preacher.

43

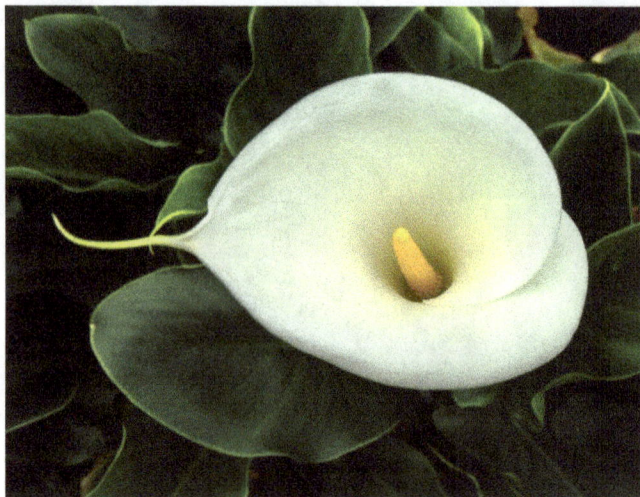

Calla lily or water arum

Jack-in-the-pulpit prefers wet locations but is sometimes found on dry, wooded hillsides; the greater abundance of blossoms occurs in late May. This plant has another name, which it earned by being interesting below ground as well as above. It has a solid, flattened, food-storehouse called a corm with a fringe of coarse rootlets encircling its upper portion. This corm was used as a food by the Indians, which fact gave the plant the name of Indian turnip. I think all children test the corm as a food for curiosity, and retire from the field with a new respect for the stoicism of the Indian when enduring torture; but this is an undeserved tribute. When raw, these corms are peppery because they are filled with minute, needle-like spicules which, however, soften with boiling, and the Indians boiled them before eating them.

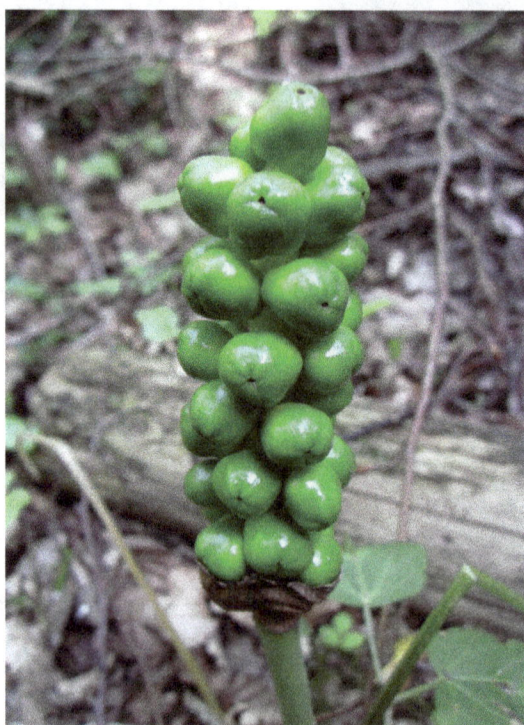

The berries of Jack-in-the-pulpit

Jack-in-the-pulpit is a near cousin to the calla lily; the white part of the calla and the striped hood over "Jack" are both spathes, and a spathe is a leaf modified for the protection of a flower or flowers. "Jack" has but one leg and his flowers are set around it, all safely enfolded in

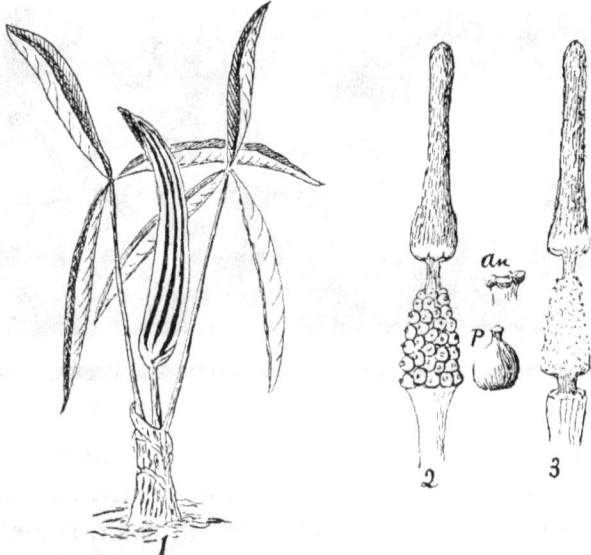

1. *Jack-in-the-pulpit unfolding;* 2. *Spadix with pistillate flowers;* 3. *Spadix with staminate flowers;* P. Pistillate flower enlarged; An, a staminate flower enlarged, showing the four anthers.

the lower part of the spathe. The pistillate flowers which make the berries are round and greenish, and are packed like berries on the stalk; they have purple stigmas with whitish centers. The pollen-bearing flowers are mere little projections, almost white in color, each usually bearing four purplish, cup-like anthers filled with white pollen. Occasionally both kinds of flowers may be found on one spadix, (as "Jack" is called in the botanies), the pollen-bearing flowers being set above the others; but usually they are on separate plants. Professor Atkinson has demonstrated that when a plant becomes very strong and thrifty, its spadix will be set with the pistillate flowers and its berries will be many; but if the same plant becomes weak, it produces the pollen-bearing flowers the next year.

When "Jack" first appears in the spring it looks like a mottled, pointed peg, for it is well sheathed. Within this sheath the leaves are rolled lengthwise to a point, and at the very center of the rolled leaves is a spathe, also rolled lengthwise, and holding at its heart the developing flower-buds. It is a most interesting process to watch the unfolding of one of these plants. On the older plants there are two, or sometimes three leaves, each with three large leaflets; on the younger

45

Border design featuring Jack-in-the-pulpit

plants there may be but one of these compound leaves, but the leaflets are so large that they seem like three entire leaves.

The spathes, or pulpits, vary in color, some being maroon and white or greenish, and some greenish and white. They are very pretty objects for water-color drawings.

Small flies and some beetles seem to be the pollen carriers for this plant. Various ingenious theories have been suggested to prove that our Jack-in-the-pulpit acts as a trap to imprison visiting insects, as does the English species; but I have studied the flowers in every stage, and have seen the insects crawl out of the hoods as easily as they crawled in, and by the same open, though somewhat narrow, passage between the spadix and the spathe.

After a time the spathe falls away showing the globular, green, shining berries. In August even the leaves may wither away, at which time the berries are brilliant scarlet. Jack-in-the-pulpit is a perennial. It does not blossom the first year after it is a seedling. I have known at least one case where blossoms were not produced until the third year. Below ground, the main corm gives off smaller corms and thus the plant spreads by this means as well as by seeds.

LESSON

Leading thought— The real flowers of Jack-in-the-pulpit are hidden by the striped spathe which is usually spoken of as the flower. This plant has a peppery root which the Indians used for food.

Method— The questions should be answered from observation in the woods; a single plant may be dug up and brought to school for study, and later planted in some shady spot in the school garden.

Observations—

1. Where do you find Jack-in-the-pulpit? Is the soil dry or damp? Do you ever find it in the fields?

2. How early in the season does this plant blossom? How late?

3. How does the Jack-in-the-pulpit look when it first pushes out from the ground? How are its leaves rolled in its spring overcoat?

4. How does the pulpit, or spathe, look when the plant first unfolds? Is its tip bent over or is it straight?

5. Describe or sketch the leaves of Jack-in-the-pulpit. How do they rise above and protect the flower? How many leaflets has each leaf? Sketch the leaflets to show the venation. How do these stand above the flower? Can you find any of the plants with only one leaf?

6. Why is the spathe called a pulpit? What are the colors of the spathe? Are all the spathes of the same colors?

7. Open up the spathe and see the rows of blossoms around the base of the spadix, or if you call the spadix, "Jack," then the flowers clothe his one leg. Are all the blossoms alike? Describe, if you can, those flowers which will produce the seed and those which produce the pollen. Do you find the two on the same spadix or on different plants?

8. What insects do you find carrying the pollen for "Jack?" Do you know how its seeds look in June? How do they look in August? Do the leaves last as long as the seeds?

9. What sort of a root has "Jack?" How does it taste? Do you think the Indians boiled it before they ate it? What other name has "Jack?" How does the plant multiply below the ground?

10. Compare the Jack-in-the-pulpit with the calla lily.

11. Write an English theme on "The Sermon that Jack Preached from His Pulpit."

Common violet

The Violet

TEACHER'S STORY

It is interesting to note the flowers which have impinged upon the imagination of the poets; the violet more than most flowers has been loved by them, and they have sung in varied strains of its fragrance and lowliness.

Browning says:

> *"Such a starved bank of moss,*
> *'Till that May morn,*
> *Blue ran the flash across;*
> *Violets were born."*

And Wordsworth sings:

> *"A violet by a mossy stone,*
> *Half hidden from the eye;*
> *Fair as a star, when only one*
> *Is shining in the sky."*

Cultivated violas

And Barry Cornwall declares that the violet

"Stands first with most, but always with the lover."

But Shakespeare's tribute is the most glowing of all, since the charms of both the goddesses of beauty and of love are made to pay tribute to it:

"Violets dim,
But sweeter than the lids
of Juno's eyes,
Or Cytherea's breath."

However, the violets go on living their own lives, in their own way, quite unmindful of the poets. There are many different species, and they frequent quite different locations. Some live in the woods, others in meadows and others in damp, marshy ground. They are divided into two distinct groups—those where the leaf-stems come directly from the root, and those where the leaves come from a common stem, the latter being called the leafy-stemmed violets. Much attention

Opened seed capsule of Viola arvensis

should be given to sketching and studying the leaf accurately of the specimens under observation, for the differences in the shapes of the leaves, in many instances, determine the species; in some cases the size and shape of the stipules determines the species; and whether the leaves and stems are downy or smooth is another important characteristic. In the case of those species where the leaves spring from the root, the flower stems rise from the same situation; but in the leafy-stemmed violets the flower stems come off at the axils of the leaves. In some species the flower stems are long enough to lift the flowers far above the foliage, while in others they are so short that the flowers are hidden.

The violet has five sepals and their shape and length is a distinguishing mark. There are five petals, one pair above, one at each side, and a broad lower petal which gives the bees and butterflies a resting place when they are seeking nectar. This lower petal is prolonged backward into a spur which holds the nectar.

The spur forms the nectary of the violet, and in order to reach the sweet treasure, which is at the rearmost point of the nectary, the insect must thrust its tongue through a little door guarded by both anthers and pistil; the insect thus becomes laden with pollen, and carries it from flower to flower. In many of the species, the side petals have at their bases a little fringe which forms an arch over the door or throat leading to the nectary. While this is considered a guard to keep out undesirable insects like ants, I am convinced that it is also useful in brushing the pollen from the tongues of the insect visitors.

Some species of violets are very fragrant, while others have little odor. The color of the anthers also differs with different species. The children should be interested in watching the development of the seeds from the flower. The seed-pods are three-lobed, each one of these lobes dividing lengthwise, with a double row of seeds within. Each lobe curls back and thus scatters the seed.

At the base of most of the species of violets can be found the small flowers which never open; they have no petals, but within them the pollen and the pistil are fully developed. The flowers seem to be developed purposely for self-pollenation, and in the botanies they are called cleistogamous flowers; in some species they are on upright stems, in others they lie flat.

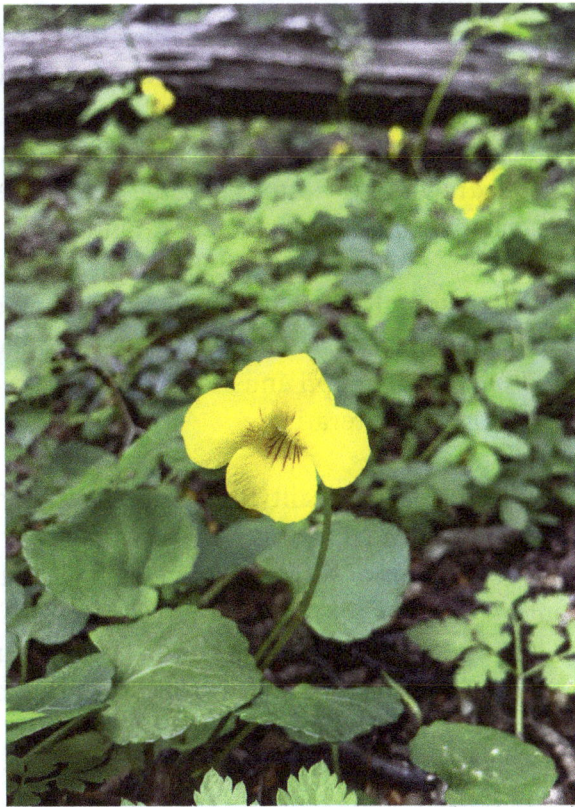

Yellow violet

There is much difference in the shape of the rootstock in the different species of violet; some are delicate and others are strong, and some are creeping.

LESSON

Leading thought— Each violet flower has a well of nectar, with lines pointing to it so that the insects may find it. They also have down near their roots, flowers which never open, which are self-pollenated and develop seeds.

Method— To make this work of the greatest use and interest, each pupil should make a portfolio of the violets of the locality. This may be in the form of pressed and mounted specimens, or of water-color drawings. In either case, the leaf, leaf-stem, flower, flower stem, and rootstock should be shown, and each blossom should be neatly labelled with name, locality and date. From the nature-study standpoint, a portfolio of drawings is the more desirable, since from making the drawings the pupils become more observant of the differences in structure and color which distinguish the species. Such a portfolio may be a most beautiful object; the cover of thick cardboard may have an original, conventionalized design made from the flowers and leaves of the violets. Each drawing may be followed by a page containing notes by the pupil and some appropriate quotation from botany, poetry or other literature.

Observations—

1. Describe the locality and general nature of the soil where the violet was found. That is, was it in the woods, dry fields or near a stream?

2. Sketch or describe the shape of the leaf, paying particular attention to its margin and noting whether it is rolled toward the stem at its base. Is the petiole longer or shorter than the leaf? Does the leaf stem spring directly from the root, or does it branch from another? If the latter, are the leaves opposite or alternate? Is there a stipule where the leaf joins the main stem? If so, is it toothed on the edge?

3. What is the color of the leaf above? Are the leaves and stems downy and velvety, or smooth and glossy?

4. Does the flower stem come from the root of the plant, or does it grow from the main stem at the axil of the leaf? Are the flower stems long enough to lift the flowers above the foliage of the plant?

5. How many sepals has the violet? Are they long or short; pointed or rounded? How many petals has the violet? How are they arranged? Is the lower petal shaped like the others? What is the use of this broad lower petal? Are there any marks upon it? If you should follow one of these lines, where would it lead to?

6. Look at the spur at the back of the flower. Of which petal is it a part? How long is it, compared with the whole flower? What is the use of this spur?

7. Find the door that leads to the nectar-spur and note what the tongue of the bee or butterfly would brush against when reaching for the nectar. Are the side petals which form the arch over the door that

DWERGENPAARTJE (CC BY-SA 4.0)

Viola decumbens

leads to the nectar fringed at their bases? If so, what is the use of this fringe?

8. What colors are the petals? Are they the same on both sides? How are they marked and veined? Are the flowers fragrant?

9. What color are the anthers? What color is the stigma? Examine a fading violet, and describe how the seed is developed from the flower.

10. Find the seed-pods of the violet. How are the seeds arranged within them? How do the pods open? How are the seeds scattered?

11. Look at the base of the violet and find the little flowers there which never open. Examine one of these flowers and find if it has sepals, petals, anthers and pistil. Are these closed flowers on upright stems or do the stems lie flat on the earth? Of what use to the plant are these little closed flowers?

12. What sort of rootstock has the violet? Is it short and thick or slender? Is it erect, oblique or creeping?

The May Apple, or Mandrake

TEACHER'S STORY

THIS is a study of parasols and, therefore, of perennial interest to the little girls who use the small ones for their dolls, and with many airs and graces hold the large ones above their own heads. And when this diversion palls, they make mandarin dolls of these fascinating plants. This is easily done by taking one of the small plant umbrellas and tying with a grass-sash all but two of the lobes closely around the stem, thus making a dress, the lobes left out being cut in proper shape for flowing sleeves; then for a head some other flower is robbed of its flower bud, which is put into place and surmounted with a clover leaflet hat, and a pin is then thrust through hat, head and neck into the stem of the dressed plant; the whole is properly finished by placing a small umbrella above the little green mandarin.

The mandrakes grow in open places where there is sun, and yet not too much of it; they like plenty of moisture, and grow luxuriantly in open glades or in meadows or pastures bordering woodlands, and they especially rejoice in the fence-corners, along roadsides. The first lesson of all should be how nature folds her little umbrellas. Study the plants when they first put their heads above ground, each parasol wrapped in its case, and note how similarly to a real umbrella it is folded around its stem. Later, after the umbrellas are fairly spread, they afford a most interesting study in varieties of form and size. Some of the parasols have only four lobes while others have many more. I have found them with as many as nine, although the botanies declare seven to be the normal number. One of the special joys afforded by nature-study is finding things different from the descriptions of them in the books.

One of these little parasols is a worthy object for careful observation. Its stem is stout and solid, and at its base may be seen the umbrella-case, now discarded like other umbrella-cases; the stem is pink wherever the sun touches it, but close up under the leaves it is likely to be green; it ends at the middle of the parasol by sending out strong, pale green, fuzzy ribs into each lobe. The lobes are narrow toward the stem but broad at the outer edge, each lobe being sparsely toothed on its outer margins and with a deep, smooth notch at the center. From the ribs of each lobe extend other ribs, an arrangement quite different from that we find in cloth umbrellas. The lobes of the mandrake parasol are divided almost to the center, and it is therefore evident that it is much better fitted for protection from the sun than from the rain. The parasol is a beautiful shining green on the upper side, and has a pale green lining that feels somewhat woolly.

In examining any patch of May apples, we find that many of the parasols are double; the secret of this is, that the mandrake baby needs two parasols to shield it from the sun; one of these twin parasols is always larger than the other and evidently belongs to the main stem, since its stem is stouter, and it is likely to have seven lobes while the smaller one may have but five. However, the number of lobes varies. Neither of these double parasols has its ribs extending out toward the other, and thus interfering; instead of having their "sticks" at the center of the parasol, they are at the side next each other, exactly as if the

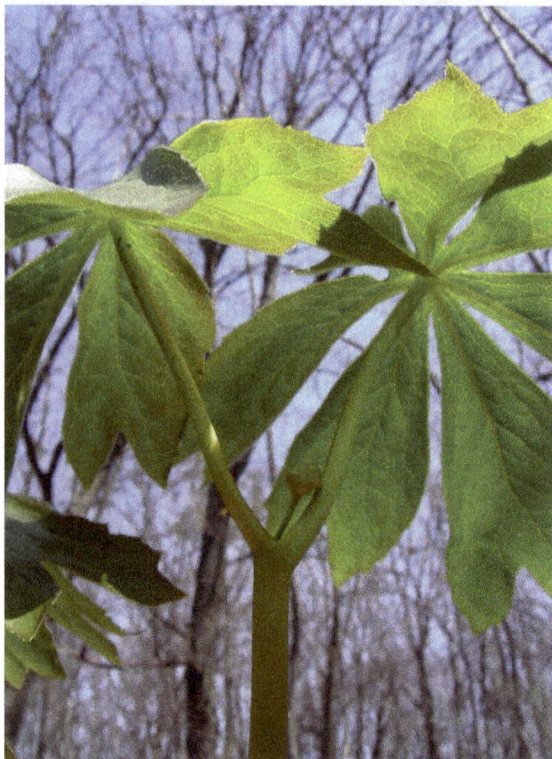

May apple leaves

original single stem had been split and the whole parasol had been torn in twain.

But of greatest interest is the blossom-baby carried under this double parasol. At first it is a little, elongate, green ball on a rather stiff little stem, which droops because it wants to and not because it has to, and which arises just where the two branches fork. One of the strange things about this precocious baby-bud is, that when the plant is just coming from the ground, the bud pushes its head out from between the two folded parasols, and takes a look at the world before it retires under its green sunshade. As the bud unfolds, it looks as if it had three green sepals, each keeping its cup form and soon falling off, as a little girl drops her hood on a warm day; but each of these sepals, if examined, will be found to be two instead of one; the outer is the outside of the green hood while the inner is a soft, whitish membrane,

"A rabbit skin,
To wrap the Baby Bunting in."

As the greenish white petals spread out, they disclose a triangular mass of yellow stamens grouped about the big seed-box, each side of the triangle being opposite one of the inner petals. After the flower is fully open, the stamens spread and each anther is easily seen to be grooved, and each edge of the groove opens for the whole of its length; but because of its shape and position, it lets the pollen fall away from the pistil instead of toward it; nor do the tips of the anthers reach the waxy, white, ruffled stigma. There is no nectar in this flower; but the big queen bumblebee likes the pollen for her new nest, and she "bumbles" around in the flower while getting her load, so that she becomes well dusted with the pollen, and thus carries it from flower to flower. But the whole story of the pollen carriers of the May apple is, as yet, untold; and any child who is willing to give time and attention to discovering the different insects which visit this flower, may give to the world valuable and, as yet, unknown facts. It is said that a white moth is often found hanging to the flowers, but it is difficult to understand why the moth should be there if the flower does not have any nectar.

The seed-vessel at the center of the flower is large and chunky, and, although crowned with its ruffled stigma, looks as if it were surely going to "grow up" into a May apple. There are usually six wide, white, rounded petals, three on the outside and three on the inside; but sometimes there are as many as nine. There are usually twice as many stamens as petals, but I have often found thirteen stamens, which is not twice any possible number of petals. The petals soon fall, and, safely hidden from the eyes of enemies, the green fruit—which is a berry instead of an apple—has nothing to do but gather sweetness, until in July it is as juicy and luscious to the thirsty child as if it were the fruit of the gods. It is about two inches long, a rich yellow in color, and is sometimes called the "wild lemon," although it is not sour. It is also called the hog-apple because the clever swine of the South know how to find it, despite its parasol. Riley thus celebrates this fruit:

> "And will any poet sing of a lusher, richer thing,
> Than a ripe May apple, rolled like a pulpy lump of gold
> Under thumb and finger tips; and poured molten through the lips?"

If the May apple itself is edible, certainly its root is not, except when given by physicians as a medicine, for it is quite poisonous when eaten. When we see plants growing in colonies or patches, it usually means that very interesting things are going on underground beneath them, and the mandrake is no exception to this. Each plant has a running underground stem, straight and brown and fairly smooth; at intervals of a few inches, there are attached to it rosettes of stout, white roots, which divide into tiny, crooked rootlets. There is a large rosette of these roots under the plant we are studying, and we can always find a rosette of them under the place where the plant stood last year. Beneath the present plant we can find the bud from which will grow the root-stem for the coming year. The working out of the branching and the peculiarities of these root-stems, is an excellent lesson in this peculiar and interesting kind of plant reproduction.

LESSON

Leading thought— These interesting plants grow in colonies because of the spreading of their underground stems. Their odor and poisonous qualities protect them from being eaten by animals, and their fruit is well hidden by its green parasol until it is ripe.

Method— Begin the study just as the mandrakes are thrusting their heads up through the soil in April, and continue the work at intervals until the fruit is ripe.

Observations—

1. How do the mandrakes look when they first appear above the ground? How are the little umbrellas folded in their cases? What do the cases look like? How can you tell from the first, the plants which are to bear the flowers and fruit?

2. Study a patch of mandrakes, and see how many varieties of parasols you can find. Do they all have the same number of main ribs and lobes? How many lobes do most of them have? Are there more single or double parasols in the patch?

3. Take a single plant and study it carefully. What sort of stem has it? Can you find at its base the old umbrella case? How high is the stem? What is its color at the bottom and at the top? How many ribs does it divide into at the top? Are these ribs as smooth as the stem? How does the parasol lining differ from its outside in color and feeling?

4. Study the parasol lobes. What is their general shape? Are they all notched at the wide end? How close to the stem does the division between them extend? Do you not think they are better fitted for keeping off the sun than the rain?

5. Take one of the double parasols. Where is the flower bud to be

found? How is it protected from the sun? Does the stem divide equally on each side of it or is one part larger than the other? Are the twin parasols of the same size? How many lobes has each? What are the chief differences in shape between one of these twin parasols and one of the parasols which has no flower bud?

6. How does the flower bud look? Does it droop because its stem is weak? What happens to the green hood or sepals when the flower opens? Can you find six sepals in the hood?

May apple, showing flowers and leaves

7. Does the open flower bow downward? As the flower opens, what is the shape of the group of stamens at the center? Are there the same number of white, waxy petals in all the flowers? Are there always about twice as many stamens as petals? How do the anthers open to shed the pollen? Do they let the pollen fall away from the ruffled stigma of the "fat" little seed box at the center of the flower?

8. Does the flower have a strong odor? Does not the plant itself give off this odor? Do you think it is pleasant? Do the cattle eat the mandrake when it is in pastures?

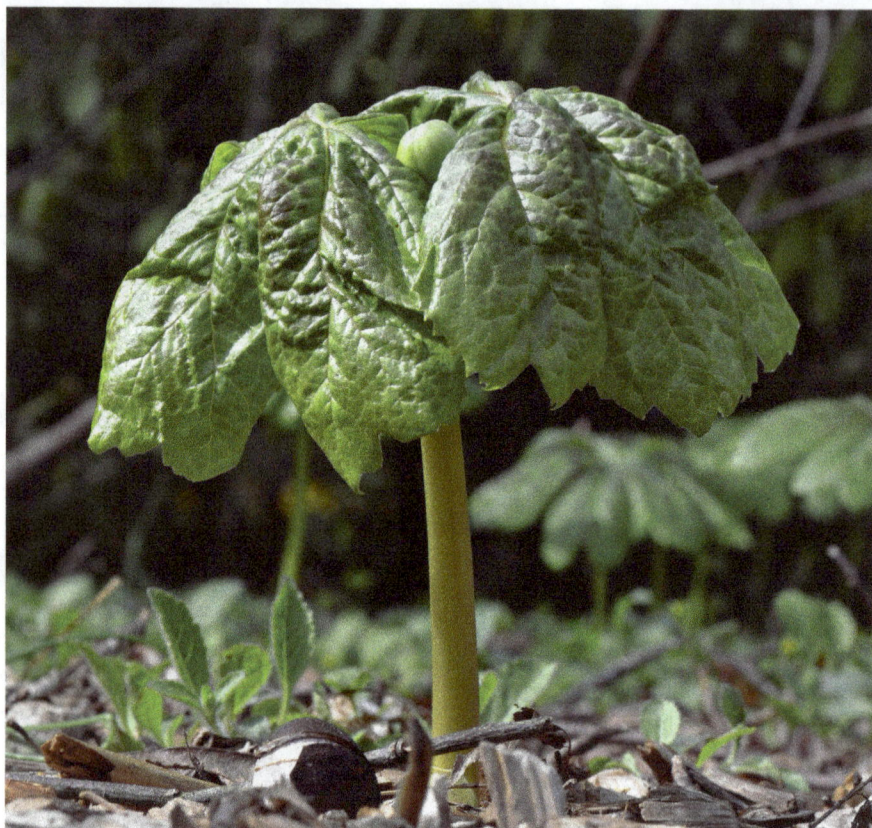

May apple fruit

9. What insects do you find visiting the mandrake flowers?

10. Do you like the May apple? When is it ripe? Cut a fruit across and see how the seeds are arranged.

11. Where are mandrakes found? Do they always grow in patches? Dig up a few plants and find why this is so.

12. Describe the underground stem. Can you find where the last year's plant grew? How are the roots arranged upon the stem? Can you see places which will produce the stem for next year's growth? How does the underground stem differ in appearance from the true roots? Why must we not taste of the mandrake root?

13. In late July, visit the mandrake patch again. Are there any umbrellas now? What is left of the plants? Look at the underground stems again and see if there are new growths, and if they are larger and stored with food for next year's plants.

The Bluets

DURING April, great patches of blue appear in certain meadows, seeming almost like reflections from the sky; and yet when we look closely at the flowers which give this azure hue to the fields, we find that they are more lavender than blue. The corolla of the bluet is a tube, spreading out into four long, lavender, petal-like lobes; each lobe is paler toward its base and the opening of the tube has a ring of vivid yellow about it, the tube itself being yellow even to its very base, where the four delicate sepals clasp it fast to the ovary until the flower has done its work; and after the corolla has fallen the sepals remain; standing guard over the growing seed.

If we look carefully at the bluets we find two forms of flowers: (a) Those with a two-lobed stigma protruding from the opening of the flower tube. (b) Those where the throat of the tube seems closed by four anthers which join like four fingertips pressed together. In opening the flower, we observe that those which have the stigmas protruding from the tube, have four anthers fastened to the sides of the tube

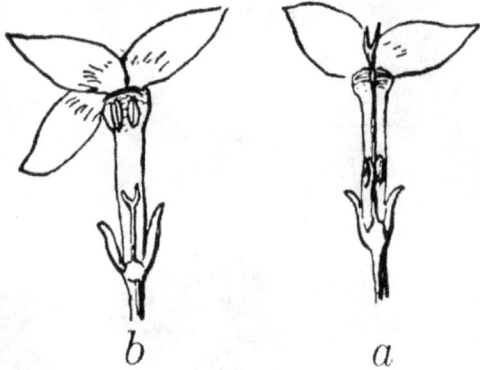

1. Section of a bluet blossom that has the anthers at the throat of the tube and the stigmas below. 2. Section of a bluet with the stigmas protruding and the anthers below.

about half-way down; while those that have the four anthers near the opening of the tube, have a pistil with a short style which brings the stigmas about half-way up the tube. Thus an insect visiting flower (a) gets her tongue dusted with pollen from the anthers at the middle of the tube; and this pollen is applied at exactly the right place on her tongue to brush off against the stigmas of a flower of the (b) form. While a bee visiting a bluet of the (b) form receives the pollen at the base of her tongue, where it is conveniently placed to be brushed off by the protruding stigmas of the flowers of the (a) form.

This arrangement in flowers for the reciprocal exchange of pollen characterizes members of the primrose family also; it is certainly a very clever arrangement for securing cross-pollenation.

LESSON

Leading thought— The bluets have two forms of flowers, the anthers and stigmas being placed in different positions in the two, in order to secure cross-pollination by visiting insects.

Method— Ask the children to bring in several bits of sod covered with bluets. During recess let the pupils, with the aid of a lens if necessary, find the two different forms of flowers. Later, let each see a flower of each form with the tube opened lengthwise.

Observations—

1. Where do the bluets grow? Do they grow singly or in masses? On what kind of soil do they grow, in woods or meadows? At what time of year do they bloom?

2. Describe the bluet flower, its color, the shape of its sepals, the

form of the corolla, the color of the corolla-tube and lobes.

3. Where is the nectar in the bluet? What color shows where the nectar is to be found?

4. Look directly into the flowers. Do you see any with the stigmas thrust out of the corolla-tube? Is there more than one style? Has it one or two stigmas? Open this flower-tube and describe where the anthers are situated in it. How many anthers are there?

5. Look for a flower where the stigmas do not protrude and the anthers close the throat of the tube. Where are the stigmas in this flower, below or above the anthers? Where are the anthers attached?

6. Work out this problem: How do the insects gathering nectar from one form of the bluets become dusted with pollen in such a way as to leave it upon the stigma of the other form of the bluet flower?

7. How many sepals are there? Do they fall off when the blossom falls?

> "So frail, these smiling babies,
> Near mossy pasture bars,
> Where the bloodroot now so coyly
> Puts forth her snowy stars;
> And the maple tall and slender,
> With blossoms red and sweet,
> Looks down upon the bluets
> Close nestled at her feet.
> 'Innocents', the children call them,—
> These floral babies small,
> Of Mother Nature olden,
> Whose broad lap holds them all."

—RAY LAURANCE.

The Yellow Lady's Slipper

TEACHER'S STORY

"Graceful and tall the slender drooping stem,
With two broad leaves below,
Shapely the flower so lightly poised between,
And warm its rosy glow."

—ELAINE GOODALE.

These showy flowers look so strange in our woodlands that we gaze at them as curiously as we might upon a veiled lady from the Orient who had settled in our midst. There is something abnormal and mysterious in the shape of this flower, and though it be called the lady's slipper, yet it would be a strange foot that could fit such a slipper; and if it is strange at the first glance, it is still more so as we try to compare it with other flowers. There are two long sepals that extend up and down, the lower one being made up of two grown together—but the "seam" does not show. The sepals are yellow, and are wider than the two long streamers that extend out at right angles to them, and which are petals; the brighter color of the latter, their markings of reddish dots, the hairs near their bases, all go to show that these petals, although so different in shape, belong to the same series as the big lower petal which is puffed out into a sac, shaped like a deep, long bowl, with its upper edges incurved. If we look carefully at this bowl, we find two openings besides the main one; these two are near the stem, and their edges are not incurved. Extending out into each of these openings is a strange little round object, which is an anther; but if we try to get pollen from this anther with a pencil or a knife we get, instead of powdery pollen, a smear that sticks to what it touches, like melted rubber or gum. The secret of this is, that the lower side of the anther is gummy, and adheres to whatever touches it and brings with it, when pulled away, the mealy pollen which lies loose above it. Another strange thing is that, if this lower part of the anther is not carried away, it seems to partially harden and opens downward, letting the pollen escape in a way usual with other flowers. We have to remove a side of the bowl to see the stigma; it is fan-shaped, and is bent at right angles to the flower stem; and above it, as if to protect it, is a stiff triangular piece which is really a strangely modified stamen. I think one reason why the lady's slipper always is called "she" is because of this tendency on her part to divert an object from its natural use. Surely a hairpin used for a paper knife or a monkey-wrench for a hammer, is not nearly so feminine a diversion as a stamen grown wide and long to make an awning above a stigma.

The general color of the flower is yellow, and there are some seductive dark red spots on the stamen-awning and along the folded-in surface of the petal-sac which say plainly, "Come here, Madam Mining-bee, and see what these spots mean." And the little bee alights on the flower and soon crawls into the well at the center, the recurved edges preventing it from returning by the same door. At the bottom of the sac there are delectable vegetable hairs to be browsed upon; if there is nectar, I have never been able to detect it with my coarse organs of taste; and Mr. Eugene Barker, who has examined hundreds of the flowers, has not been able to detect the presence of nectar in them at any stage; but he made no histological study of the glands.

After a satisfying meal the bee, which is a lively crawler, seeks to get out where it sees the light shining through one of the openings near to the stem. In doing this, she presses her head and back, first against the project- ing stigma and then against the sticky an- ther, which smears her with a queer kind of plaster; and it sticks there until she brushes it off on the stigma of another flower, when crowd- ing past it; and there she again becomes smeared with pollen plaster from this flower's anthers. Mr. Barker, who has especially studied these flowers, has found that the little min- ing bees of the genus *Andrena* were the most frequent visitors; he also found honey-bees and one stray young grasshopper in the sacs. The mining bees which he sent to me had their backs plastered with the pollen. Mr. Barker states that the flowers are not visited frequently by insects, and adds feelingly: "My long waiting was rewarded with little insect activity, aside from the mosquitoes which furnished plenty of entertainment."

The ovary looks like a widened and ribbed portion of the flower- stem, and is hairy outside; its walls are thick and obscurely three- angled; seen in cross-section the seeds are arranged in a triangular fashion which is very pretty.

The leaves of the yellow lady's slipper are oval or elliptic, with

Lady's Slipper in their native habitat

smooth edges and parallel veins; they often have narrow veins between each two heavier ones. The leaves are of vivid yellowish green and are scattered, in a picturesque manner, alternately along the stem, which their bases completely clasp. The stem is somewhat rough and ribbed and is likely to grow crooked; it grows from one to two feet in height. The roots are a mass of small rootlets. The species is found in woods and in thickets.

The pink moccasin flower, also called the stemless lady's slipper (*C. acaule*), is perhaps prettier than the yellow species, and differs from it in several particulars. The sac opens by the merest crevice, and there are plenty of dark-pink guiding lines which lead to the little opening of the well. The downward-folded edges prevent the visiting insect from getting out by this door even more surely than in the other species. The side petals are not so long as in the yellow species, and they extend forward as if to guide the insect to the well in the lower petal. The sepals are greenish purple, and are likewise shorter; and the lower one is wide, indicating that it is made up of two grown together. At the base of the ovary there is a pointed green bract or leaf, which lifts up and bends above the flower. There are but two leaves on the stemless

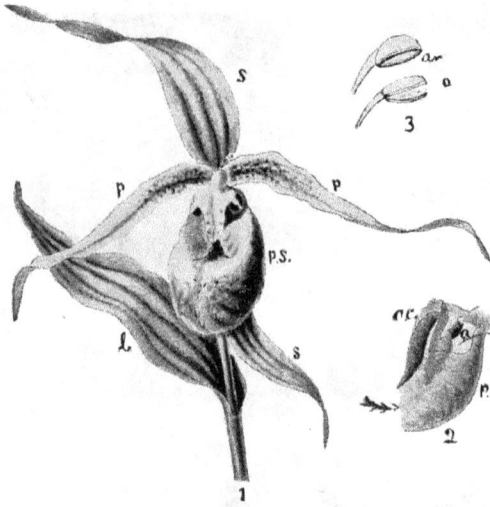

lady's slipper; they arise from the base of the stem. They are broadly ovate, and from six to seven inches long. This species grows in sandy or rocky woods.

Another species more beautiful than these is the showy lady's slipper, which is white with a pink entrance to the petal sac. This grows in peaty bogs, and is not so common as the others.

Detail of yellow lady's-slipper
1, 1, leaf; s,s, sepals; p.p, petals; p.,s., petal sac. 2, Side view: a.c., anther cover; p.s., petal sac; a, anther. 3, an, anther closed; o, anther open

The interesting points for observation in these flowers are the careful noting of the kinds of insects which visit them, and how they enter and leave the "slipper," or sac.

LESSON

Leading thought— The moccasin flower belongs to that family of flowers known as orchids which especially depend upon insects for bringing and carrying pollen, and which have developed many strange devices to secure insect aid in pollenation.

Method— A bouquet of lady's slippers should be brought to the schoolroom. Children who bring them should describe the place where they were found.

Observations—

1. Where does the yellow lady's slipper grow? Look carefully at its leaves and describe them. How do they join the stem? Are they opposite or alternate?

2. What is there peculiar about the sepals? How many are there?

3. Describe the three petals and the difference and likeness in their form and color. What is the shape of the lower petal? Is there a hole in

this sac? Is there more than one hole leading into it? What is the color of the sac? Is there anything about it to attract insects? If an insect should enter the mouth of the well in the lower petal could it easily come out by the same opening? Why not? Where do you think it would emerge?

4. Note the two roundish objects projecting into the two openings of the sac near the stem. Thrust a pencil against the under side of one of these. What happens? How does this pollen differ from the pollen of ordinary flowers?

5. Cut away one side of the petal-sac and find the stigma. What shape is it? Where is it situated with relation to the anthers? How is the stigma protected above? Where is the ovary, or seed-box?

6. Explain how a bee visiting these flowers, one after another, must carry the pollen from one to another and deposit it on the waiting stigmas.

7. How is the insect attracted? How is it trapped and made to do the work?

8. Look at the seed-capsule and describe it from the outside. Cut it across, and describe the arrangement of the seeds. How many sides of the seed-capsule open, to let loose the seeds?

9. How many species of lady's slippers do you know? Do you know the pink, or stemless species? How does it differ from the yellow species in the following particulars: The shape of the sac; its color and markings; the length and shape of sepals; the number and position of the leaves.

The Evening Primrose

TEACHER'S STORY

"Children came
To watch the primrose blow. Silent they stood,
Hand clasped in hand, in breathless hush around,
And saw her shyly doff her soft green hood
And blossom—with a silken burst of sound."

—MARGARET DELAND.

To the one who has seen the evening primrose unfold, life is richer by a beautiful, mysterious experience. Although it may be no more wonderful than the unfolding of any other flower, yet the suddenness of it makes it seem more marvelous. For two or three days it may have been getting ready; the long tube which looks like the flower stem has been turning yellow; pushing up between two of the sepals, which clasp tips beyond it, there appears a row of petals. Then some warm evening, usually about sunset, but varying from four o'clock in the afternoon to nine or ten in the evening, the petals begin to unfurl; they are wrapped around each other in the bud as an umbrella is folded, and thus one edge of each petal becomes free first. The petal first in freeing its edge seems to be doing all the work, but we may be sure

1. Evening primrose, showing buds, one ready to open, a flower just opened above at the left, an older flower at the right, a fading flower and seed-capsules below. 2. Seed-capsules. Cross section of seed-capsule with seeds above.

that all the others are pushing for freedom; little by little the sepals are pushed downward, until their tips, still clasped, are left beneath; and the petals now free, suddenly flare open before our delighted eyes, with a movement so rapid that it is difficult for us not to attribute to them consciousness of action. Three or four of these flowers may open on a plant the same evening; and they, with their fellows on the neighboring plants, form constellations of starry bloom that invite attention from the winged creatures of the twilight and the night. There is a difference in the time required for a primrose flower to unfold, probably depending upon its vigor; once I watched for half an hour to see it accomplished, and again I have seen it done in two or three minutes. The garden species seems to unfold more rapidly than the wild species, and is much more fragrant. The rapidity of the opening of the blossom depends upon the petals getting free from the sepals, which seem to try to repress them. The bud is long, conical, obscurely four-sided, and is completely covered by the four sepals, the tips of which are cylindrical and twisted together; this is an interesting habit, and one wonders if they hold the petals back until the latter are obliged to burst out with the force of repressed energy; after they let go of the petals, they drop below the flower angularly, and finally their tips open and each sepal turns back lengthwise along the seed-tube.

The four lemon-yellow petals are broad, with the outer margin notched. The eight stamens are stout, and set one at the middle of each petal and one between each two petals. The long, pale yellow anthers discharge their pollen in cobwebby strings. When the flower first opens, the stigma is egg-shaped and lies below the anthers; later, it opens into a cross and usually hangs off at one side of the anthers. If we try to trace the style back to the ovary, we find that it extends down into what seems to be the very base of the flower stem, where it joins the main stem. This base is enlarged and ribbed and is the seed-box, or ovary. The tube is rich in nectar, but only the long sucking-tubes of moths can reach it, although I have sometimes seen the ubiquitous bees attempting it. The butterflies may take the nectar in the daytime, for the blossoms of the wild species remain open, or partially open, for a day or two. But the night-flying moths which love nectar have the first chance, and it is on them the flower depends for carrying its pollen, threaded on filmy strings.

There are times when we may find the primrose blossoms with holes in the petals, which make them look very ragged. If we look at such plants carefully, we may find the culprit in the form of a green caterpillar very much resembling the green tube of the bud; and we may conclude, as Dr. Asa Fitch did, that this caterpillar is a rascal, because it crawls out on the bud-ends and nibbles into them, thus damaging several flowers. But this is only half the story. Later this caterpillar descends to the ground, digs down into it and there changes to a pupa; it remains there until the next summer, then, from this winter cell, emerges an exquisitely beautiful moth called the *Alaria florida;* its wings expand about an inch, and all except the outer edges of the front wings are rose-pink, slightly mottled with lemon-yellow, which latter color decorates the outer margins for about one-quarter of their length; the body and hind-wings are whitish and silky, the face and antennae are pinkish. Coiled up beneath the head is a long sucking-tube which may be unfolded at will. This moth is the special pollen-carrier of the evening primrose; it flies about during the evening, and thrusts its long, tubular mouth into the flower to suck the nectar, meanwhile gathering strings of pollen upon the front part of its body. During the day, it hides within the partially closed flower, thus carrying the pollen to the ripened stigmas, its colors meanwhile protecting it almost completely from observation. The fading petals of the primrose turn pink-

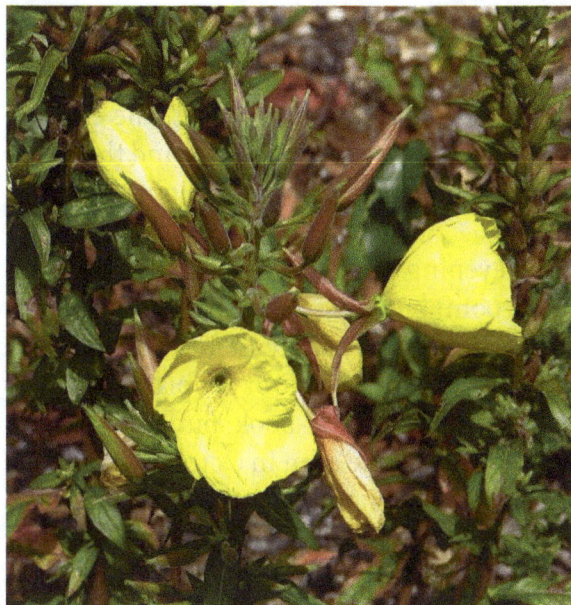

EVELYN SIMAK (CC BY-SA 2.0)

Common Evening-primrose

ish, and the pink color of the moth renders it invisible when in the old flowers, while the lemon-yellow tips of its wings protruding from a flower still fresh and yellow, forms an equally perfect protection from observation.

The evening primrose is an ornamental plant in both summer and winter. It is straight, and is ordinarily three or four feet tall, although it sometimes reaches twice that height. It is branched somewhat, the lower portion being covered with leaves and the upper portion bearing the flowers. The leaves are pointed and lanceolate, with few whitish veins. The leaf edges are somewhat ruffled and obscurely toothed, especially in the lower leaves. The leaves stand up in a peculiar way, having a short, pink petiole, which is swollen and joins the stalk like a bracket. The upper leaves are narrower; the leafy bracts at the base of the flower grow from the merest slender leaflet at the base of the bud, to a leaf as long as the seed-pod, when the flower blooms.

The seed-capsules are four-sided, long and dark green. In winter they are crowded in purplish-brown masses on the dry stalks, each one a graceful vase with four flaring tips. At the center of each there projects a needlelike point; and within the flaring, pale, satin-lined divisions of these urns, we may see the brown seeds which are tossed by the winter winds far and near. The young plants develop into vigorous rosettes during the late summer and autumn, and thus discreetly pass the winter under the snow coverlet.

LESSON

Leading thought— Some flowers have developed the habit of relying on the night-flying insects for carrying their pollen. The evening primrose is one of these; its flowers open in the evening and their pale yellow color makes them noticeable objects in the twilight, and even in the dark.

Method— The form of the evening primrose may be studied from plants brought to the schoolroom; but its special interest lies in the way its petals expand in the evening, so the study should be continued by the pupils individually in the field. This is one of the plants which is an especially fit subject for the summer note-book; but since it blossoms very late and the plants are available even in October, it is also a convenient plant to study during the school year. The garden species is well adapted for this lesson.

Observations—

1. Look at the plant as a whole. How tall is it? Is the stem stiff and straight? Where do you find it growing? Does it grow in the woods?

2. Are the leaves near the base the same shape as those at the top of the plant? What is their shape? Are the edges toothed? What is there peculiar about the veins? How do the leaves join the stem? How do the leaves look which are at the base of the flower stem? Those at the base of the buds?

3. Where on the plant do the flowers grow? Which flowers blossom first, those above or below? Take a bud nearly ready to open; what is there peculiar in the appearance of the bud stem? What is the general shape of the bud? Describe the sepals. Look at their tips carefully, and see how they hold together. Cut a bud across and see how the petals are folded within it.

4. Take an open flower; where are the sepals now? Describe the open petals, their shape and color.

5. How many stamens are there? How are they placed? What is the shape of the anthers? How does the pollen look?

6. What is the shape and the position of the stigma in the freshly opened flower? Later? Open the flower-tube and find how far down the style extends. Where is the ovary? How does the ovary look on the outside? Taste the opened tube; can you detect the nectar? What sort

of a tongue must an insect have to reach this nectar? How do the fading flowers look and act?

7. Describe the seed-pod. Cut it across, and see how many compartments there are within it. How are the seeds arranged in it? How do the pods open and how are the seeds scattered?

8. Watch the flower of the evening primrose open, and describe the process carefully. At what hour did it open? What was the movement of the petals? Can you see how they unfold in relation one to another? How do they get free from the sepals? How many minutes is required for the whole process of the opening of the flower? How many flowers on a plant expand during the same evening? Look at the open blossoms in the dark; can you see them? How do they look? What insects do you find visiting these flowers?

9. How long does the primrose blossom remain open? How do the young plants of the evening primrose pass the winter?

Supplementary reading— Blossom Hosts and Insect Guests, Gibson.

The Milkweed

TEACHER'S STORY

"Little weavers of the summer, with sunbeam shuttle bright,
And loom unseen by mortals, you are busy day and night,
Weaving fairy threads as filmy, and soft as cloud swans, seen
In broad blue sky-land rivers, above earth's fields of green."

—RAY LAURANCE.

IS there any other young plant that shows off its baby-clothes as does the young milkweed! When it comes up through the soil, each leaf is folded lengthwise around the stem, flannel side out, and it is entirely soft and white and infantile. The most striking peculiarity of the milkweed plant is its white juice, which is a kind of rubber. Let a drop of it dry on the back of the hand, and when we try to remove it we find it quite elastic and possessed of all of the qualities of crude rubber. At the first trial it seems quite impossible to tell from which part of the stem this white juice comes, but by blotting the cut end once or twice, the hollow of the center of the stem is seen to have around it a

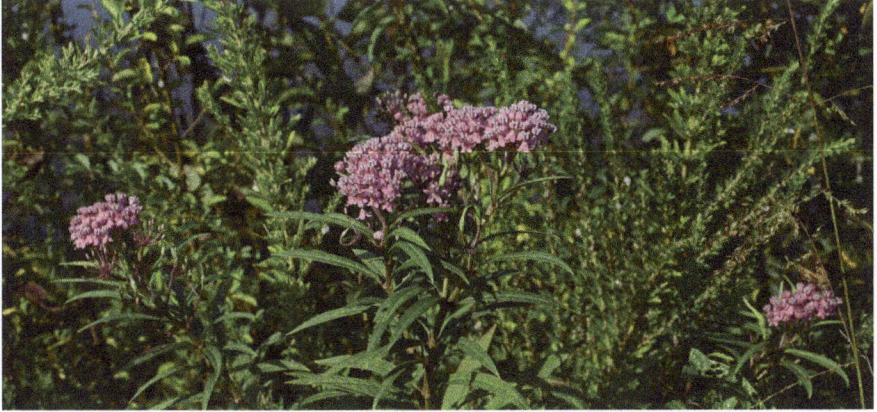
Milkweed in its natural environment

dark green ring, and outside this is a light green ring. It is from the dark green ring encircling the stem cavity that the milk exudes. This milk is not the sap of the plant any more than resin is the sap of the pine; it is a special secretion, and is very acrid to the taste, rendering milkweed disgusting to grazing animals. If a milkweed stem be broken or gashed, this juice soon heals the wound and keeps out germs, and thus is of great use to the plant, since many insects feed upon it. If cut across, every vein in every leaf produces "milk," and so does every small flower pedicel. When the "milk" is by chance smeared on cloth and allowed to dry, soap and water will not remove it, but it yields readily to chloroform, which is a solvent of rubber.

The milkweed leaves are in stately conventional pairs; if one pair points east and west, the pair above and the pair below point north and south. The leaf is beautiful in every particular; it has a dark green upper surface, diversified with veins that join in scallops near the border; it is soft to the touch on the upper surface, and is velvety below. The lens reveals that the white under surface, or the nap of the velvet, is a cover of fine white hairs.

The flower of the milkweed is too complicated for little folks even to try to understand; but for the pupils of the seventh and eighth grades it will prove an interesting subject for investigation, if they study it with the help of a lens. In examining the globular bud, we see the five hairy sepals, which are later hidden by the five long, pinkish green petals which bend back around the stem. When we look into the flower, we see five little cornucopias—which are really horns of plenty, since they are filled with nectar; from the center of each is a little, fleshy tongue, with its curved point resting on the disk at the center of the flower. Between each two of these nectar-horns can be seen the white bordered opening of a long pocket—like a dress-pocket—at the upper end of the opening of which is a black dot. Slip a needle into the pocket opening until it pushes against the black dot, and out pops a pair of yellow saddle-bags, each attached to the black dot which joins them. These are the pollen-bags, and each was borne in a sac, shaped like a vest-pocket, one lying either side of the upper end of the long pocket. These pollen-bags are sticky, and they contract so as to close over the feet of the visiting bee.

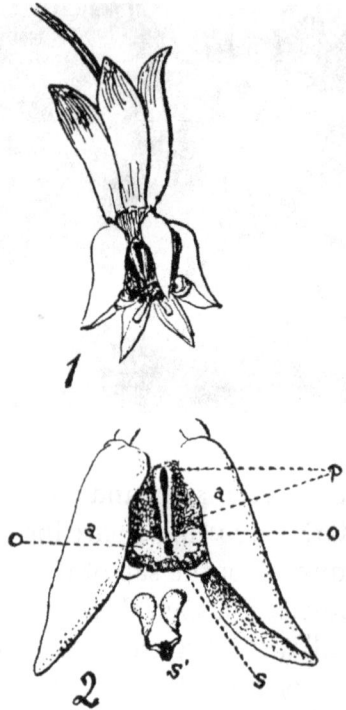

1. Milkweed flower, enlarged. 2. Same, more enlarged. a,a, nectar-horns; p, pocket; o,o, openings to the pocket; s, pollen-bags in place; s', pollen-bags removed.

Since the stem of the flower cluster droops and each flower pedicel droops, the bee is obliged to cling, hanging back down, while getting the nectar, and has to turn about as if on a pivot in order to thrust her tongue into the five cornucopias in succession; she is then certain to thrust her claws into a long pocket, and it proceeds to close upon them, its edges being like the jaws of a trap. The bee, in trying to extricate her feet, leaves whatever pollen-bags she had inadvertently gathered in this trap-pocket, which gives them passage to the stigma. But the milkweed flower, like some folks, is likely to overdo matters, and sometimes these pockets grasp too firmly the legs of the bee and hold her a prisoner. We often find insects thus caught and dead—a result as far from the plan of the flower as from that of the insect victim, had both been conscious. Sometimes bees become so covered with these pollen-bags, which they are unable to scrape off, that they die because of the clogging. But for one bee that

A milkweed pod sending forth its seed balloons

suffers there are thousands that carry off the nectar triumphantly, just as thousands of people travel by water for one that is drowned.

The milkweed pod has been the admiration of nature students from the beginning, and surely there is no plant structure that so interests the child as this house in which the milkweed carries its seeds. When we look at a green pod, we first admire its beautiful shape; on either side of the seam, which will sometime open, are three or four rows of projecting points rising from the felty surface of the pod in a way that suggests embossed embroidery. We open the pod by pulling it apart along the seam; and this is not a seam with a raw edge but is finished with a most perfect selvage. When we were children we were wont to dispossess these large green pods of their natural contents, and because they snapped shut so easily, we imprisoned therein bumblebees "to hear them sing," but we always let them go again. We now know that there is nothing so interesting as to study the contents of the pod just as it is. Below the opening is a line of white velvet; at one end, and with their "heads all in one direction," are the beautiful, pale-rimmed, brown, overlapping seeds; and at the other end we see the exquisite milkweed silk with the skein so polished that no human reel could give us a skein of such luster. If we remove the contents of the pod as a whole, we see that the velvety portion is really the seed-support and that it joins the pod at either end. It is like a hammock full of babies, except that the milkweed babies are fastened on the outside of the hammock.

No sooner is our treasure open to the air than the shining silk begins to separate into floss of fairy texture. But before one seed comes off, let us look at the beautiful pattern formed by the seeds overlapping—such patterns we may see in the mosaics of mosques.

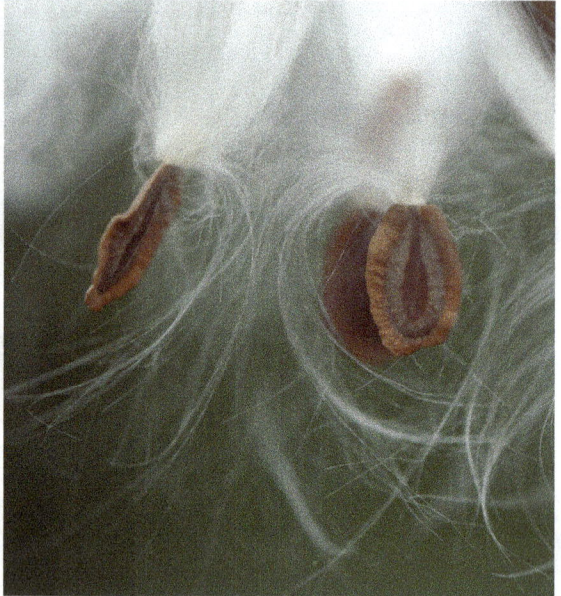

Milkweed seeds with their parachutes

Pull off a seed, and with it comes its own skein of floss, shining like a pearl; but if we hold the seed in the hand a moment the skein unwinds itself into a fluff of shining threads as fine as spiders' silk, and each individual thread thrusts itself out and rests upon the air; and altogether there are enough of the threads to float the seed, a balloon of the safest sort. If we wreck the balloon by rubbing the floss through our fingers, we shall feel the very softest textile fiber spun by Mother Nature.

If we look closely at our seed we see a margin all around it. Well, what if the balloon should be driven over sea, and the seed dropped upon the water? It must then drown unless it has a life preserver; this margin that we have noted is of the safest cork, and is warranted to float; if you do not believe it, try it.

If we pull off all the seeds, we can see that the velvety support is flat and that all of the seeds are attached to it, but before we stop our admiring study we should look carefully again at the inside of the pod, for never was there a seed cradle with a lining more soft and satiny.

LESSON

Leading thought— The milkweed when wounded secretes a milky juice which is of a rubberlike composition; it flows out of the wounded plant and soon hardens, thus protecting the wound from germs. Milkweed flowers depend entirely upon insects for pollination; the pollen is not a free, yellow powder, but it is contained in paired sacs, which are joined in V-shape. The seeds are carried by balloons, and they can float on water as well.

Method— Begin the study of the plant when it first appears above ground in April or May. Give the pupils the questions about the blossom for a vacation study, and ask that their observations be kept in their notebooks. The study of the pods and seeds may be made in September or October. When studying the milky juice, add a geography lesson on rubber trees and the way that rubber is made.

Observations—

1. *The plant*. How does the milkweed look as it appears above ground in the spring? How are its leaves folded when it first puts its head up? Cut off a fully expanded plant a few inches above the ground. What flows out of the stem? Blot off the "milk" and study the cross-section of the stem. What is at the center? How many layers do you see around this center? Can you see from which the milkweed juice comes? How

Green milkweed pods

does the juice feel as it dries on your fingers? How does it look when dry? Place a few drops on a piece of paper and when it is dry pull it off and see if it is elastic. Break the edge of the leaf. Does the milky juice flow from it? Does it come from the veins? Do you think that this is the sap of the milkweed? Cut a gash in the milkweed stem and see how the "milk" fills the wound. How does this help the plant? Do cattle feed upon the milkweed when it grows in pastures? If not, why?

2. How are the leaves arranged on the stem? How do the upper and under sides of the leaves differ? Examine with a lens, and see what makes the nap of the velvet. What gives the light color to the under side? Sketch a leaf showing its shape and venation, noting especially the direction of the veins as they approach the edge of the leaf.

3. *The flower* . Where do the flower clusters come off the stems in relation to the leaves? Does the stem of the flower cluster stand stiff or droop? Take a good sized flower cluster and count the flowers in it. What would happen if all these flowers should develop into pods? How many flower clusters do you find on one plant? Which of these clusters open first? Last?

4. Take off a single bud with its stem, or pedicel. Does the milky juice come at the break? Is the bud stem stiff or drooping? What is its

color and how does it feel? What is the shape of the bud? How many sepals has it? Look at the stem, sepals and bud with a lens and describe their covering. Look for a flower just opening where the petals stand out around it like a five-pointed star. What is their color? What happens to the petals when the flower is fully expanded? Can you see the sepals then? Look straight into the flower. Do you see the five nectar-horns? Look at them with a lens and describe them. What do you suppose is the use of the little curved tongue coming out of each? Where does the tip of the tongue rest? With a lens, look between two of the nectar horns; can you see a little slit or pocket, with white protruding edges? Note just above the pocket a black dot; thrust a needle into this pocket near its base and lift it toward the crown of the flower, touching the black dot. What happens?

5. Describe the little branched object that came out when you touched it with a needle. These are the pollen saddle-bags and each bag comes from a pocket at one side of, and above the long pocket. Do these saddlebags cling to the needle? Look with a lens at some of the older flowers, and see if you can find the pollen-bags protruding from the long pocket. See if you can find how the long pocket is a passage-way to the stigma. To see how the little saddle-bags were transported, watch a bee gathering nectar. Describe what happens.

6. Since the flowers bend over, how must the bee hold on to the flower while she gathers nectar from the horns? As she turns around, would she naturally pull out some of the saddle-bags? Catch a bee in a collecting tube and see if her feet have upon them these pollen-sacs. After gathering these pollen-sacs upon her feet, what happens to them when she visits the next flower? Is the opening of the long pocket like a trap to scrape the sacs off? Can you find on milkweed flowers any bees or other insects that have been entangled in these little traps and have thus perished? Try the experiment of drawing a thread into one of these traps and with your lens see if the opening closes over it.

7. How many kinds of insects do you find visiting the milkweed flowers? Can you detect the strong odor of the flowers? Why must the milkweed develop so many flowers and offer such an abundance of nectar?

The White Water Lily

TEACHER'S STORY
"Whence O fragrant form of light,
  Hast thou drifted through the night
  Swanlike, to a leafy nest,
  On the restless waves at rest."

Thus asks Father Tabb, and if the lily could answer it would have to say: "Through ages untold have the waves upheld me until my leaves and my flowers have changed into boats, my root to an anchor, and my stems to anchor-ropes."

There is no better example for teaching the relation between geography and plant life than the water lily. Here is a plant that has dwelt so long in a certain situation that it cannot live elsewhere. The conditions which it demands are quiet water, not too deep, and with silt bottom. Every part of the plant relies upon these conditions. The rootstock has but few root hairs; and it lies buried in the silt, not only because this gives it food, but because it can there act as an anchor. Rising from the rootstock is a stem as pliable as if made of rubber, and yet it is strong; its strength and flexibility are gained by having at its center four hollow tubular channels, and smaller channels near the outside. These tubes extend the whole length of the stem, making it light so that it will float, and at the same time giving it strength as well as flexibility. At the upper end of the stem is a leaf or flower, which is fashioned as a boat. The circular leaf is leathery and often bronze-red below, with prominent veins, making an excellent bottom to the boat; above, it is

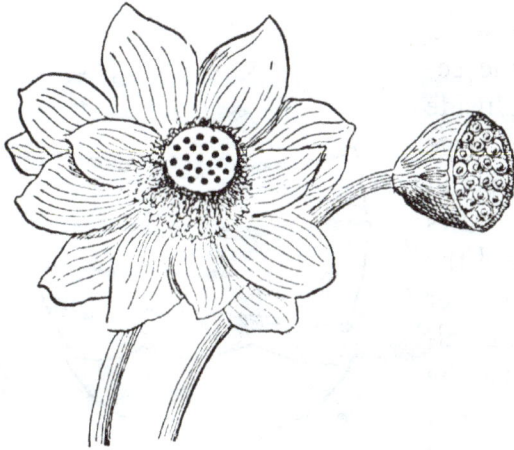
Egyptian lotus flower and seed vessel

green with a polished surface, and here are situated its breathing-pores, although the leaves of most plants have these stomata in the lower surface. But how could the water lily leaf breathe, if its stomata opened in the water? The leaf is large, circular and quite heavy; it would require a very strong, stiff stem to hold it aloft, but by its form and structure it is fitted to float upon the water, a little green dory, varnished inside, and waterproof outside.

The bud is a little, egg-shaped buoy protected by its four pink-ish brown, leathery sepals; as it opens, we can see four rows of pet-als, each overlapping the space between the next inner ones; at the

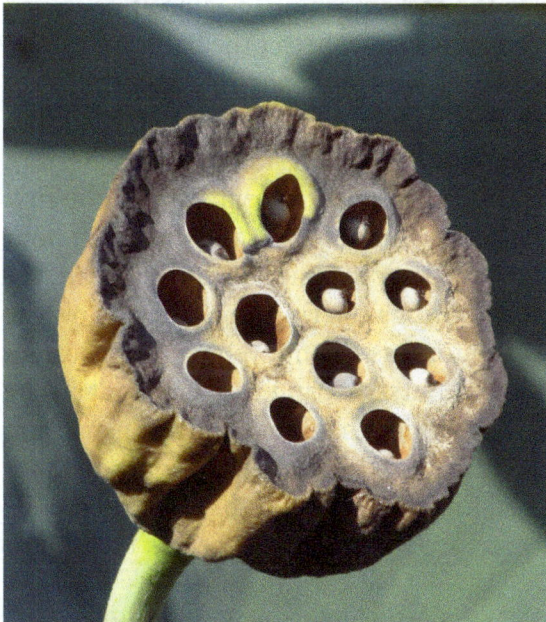
Lotus seed vessel

center there is a fine dis-play of brilliant yellow anthers. Those hanging over the greenish yellow pit, which has the stigma at its center, are merely golden hooks. When the flower is quite open, the four sepals, each a canoe in form, lie under the lily and float it; although the sepals are brown-ish outside, they are soft white on the inside next the flower. Between each two sepals stands a large petal, also canoe-shaped, and perhaps pinkish on the outside; these help the sepals in floating the flower. Inside of these there is a row of large creamy white petals which stand upright; the succeeding rows of petals are smaller toward the center and grade into the outer rows of stamens, which are petal-like at the base and pointed at the tip. The inner rows of stamens make a fine golden fringe around the cup-shaped pistil. This flower is of great use in teaching that sepals, petals and stamens have the same origin and grade into each other, showing the intermediate stages.

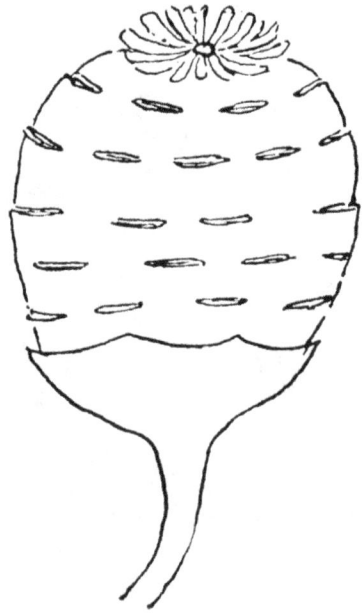

Seed vessel of white pond lily

It has been stated that pond lilies, in the state of nature, have an interesting way of opening in the early morning, closing at noon and opening again toward evening. If we knew better the habits of the insects which pollenate these flowers, we should possibly have the key to this action. In our ponds in parks and grounds we find that each species of pond lily opens and closes at its own particular time each day. Each flower opens usually for several consecutive days, and the first day of its blooming it opens about an hour later and closes an hour earlier than on the days following. After the lilies have blossomed, the flower stem coils in a spiral and brings the ripening seeds below the surface of the water. The reason for this has not yet been discovered. After about two months the pod bursts letting the seeds out in the water. Each seed is in a little bag, which the botanists call an aril, and which serves as a life preserver floating the seed off for some distance from the parent plant. The aril finally decays and the seed falls to the bottom where, if the conditions are favorable, it develops into a new plant.

To emphasize the fact that the water lily is dependent upon cer-

tain geographical conditions, ask the pupils to imagine a water lily planted upon a hillside. How could its roots, furnished with such insufficient rootlets, get nourishment there? How could its soft, flexible stems hold aloft the heavy leaves and blossoms to the sunlight? In such a situation it would be a mere drooping mass. Moreover, if the pupils understand the conditions in which the water lilies grow in their own neighborhood, they can understand the conditions under which the plant grows in other countries. Thus, when they read about the great *Victoria regia* of the Amazon,—that water lily whose leaves are large enough to support a man,—they would have visions of broad stretches of still water and they should realize that the bottom must be silt. If they read about the lotus of Egypt, then they should see the Nile as a river with borders of still water and with bottom of silt. Thus, from the conditions near at hand, we may cultivate in the child an intelligent geographical imagination.

LESSON

Leading thought— The water lily has become dependent upon certain conditions in pond or stream, and has become unfitted in form to live elsewhere. It must have quiet waters, not too deep, and with silt bottom.

Method— The study should be made first with the water lilies in a stream or pond, to discover just how they grow. For the special structure, the leaves and flowers may be brought to the schoolroom and floated in a pan of water. The lesson may easily be modified to fit the yellow water lily, which is in many ways even more interesting, since in shallow water it holds its leaves erect while in deeper water its leaves float.

Observations—

1. Where is the water lily found? If in a pond, how deep is the water? If in a stream, is it in the current? What kind of bottom is there to the stream or pond? Do you find lilies in the water of a limestone region? Why?

2. What is the shape of the leaf? What is the color above and below? What is the texture? How is it especially fitted to float? How does it look when very young?

3. Examine the petiole. How long is it? Is it stiff enough to hold up the leaf? Why does it not need to hold up the leaf? How does it serve as an anchor? Cut a stem across and describe its inside structure. How does this structure help it float?

4. Examine the open flower. How many sepals? How many rows of petals? How do the stamens resemble the petals? Can you see in the water lily how the sepals, petals and stamens may all be different forms of the same thing? How are the sepals fitted to keep the flower afloat? At what times of the day does the lily open? At what hours does it close?

5. Describe the pistil. When the lily first opens, how are the stamens placed around the pistil? What happens to the seed-box after the blossoms have faded? Does the seed-pod float upon the water as did the flower? What sort of stem has the flower? How does this stem hold the seed-pod below the water?

6. What sort of seed has the water lily? Sketch the seed-pod. How does the seed escape from it? How is it scattered and planted?

7. What sort of a root has the water lily? Are there many fine rootlets upon it? Why? How does this rootstock serve the plant aside from getting food?

8. Imagine a water lily set on a dry hillside. Could the stems uphold the flowers or leaves? Is the petiole large enough to hold out such a thick, heavy leaf? Could the root get food from a dry location? Why?

9. Judging from what you know of the places where water lilies grow and the condition of the water there, describe the Nile where the lotus grows. Describe the Amazon where the *Victoria regia* grows.

Pondweed

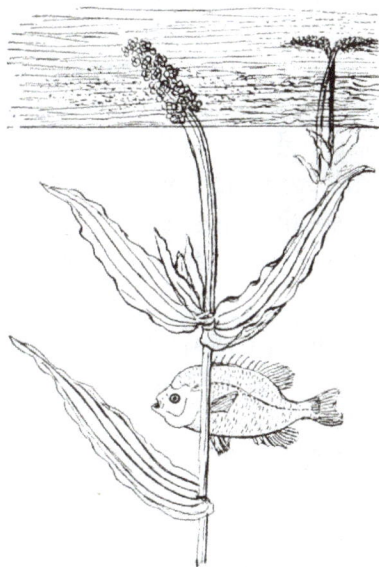

TEACHER'S STORY

HE study of any plant which has obvious limitations as to where it may grow should be made a help in the study of geography. Pondweed is an excellent subject to illustrate this principle; it grows only in quiet beds of sluggish streams or in ponds, or in the shallow protected portions of lakes. It has tremendous powers of stretching up, which render it able to grow at greater depth than one would suppose possible, often flourishing where the water is from ten to twenty feet deep. Often, when the sun is shining, it may be seen like a bed of seaweed on the bottom. Its roots, like those of most water plants, have less to do with the matter of absorbing water and nourishment than do the roots of land plants, one of their chief functions being to anchor the plant fast; they have a firm grip on the bottom; and if pondweed is cut loose, it at once comes to the surface, floats helplessly on its side, and soon dies.

The stem is very soft and pliable and the plant relies entirely on the water to keep it upright. A cross-section of the stem shows that its substance is spongy, with the larger open cells near the outer edge, thus helping it to float. The leaves are two or three inches long, their broad bases encircling the stem, their tips tapering to slender points. They have parallel veins and ruffled edges. They are dull olive green in color, much darker than the stems; in texture they are very thin, papery, and so shining as to give the impression of being varnished. No land plants have such leaves; they remind us at once of kelp or other seaweeds. The leaves are scattered along the stems, by no means thickly, for water plants do not seem to need profuse foliage.

In blossom time the pondweed shows its real beauty. The stems grow and grow, like Jack's bean stalk, and what was a bed of leaves on the pond bottom suddenly changes into a forest of high plants, each one standing tall and straight and with every leaf extended, as if its stems were as strong and stiff as ironwood; but if a wave disturbs the water the graceful undulations of the plant tell the true story of the pliant stems. There is something that arouses our admiration when we see one of these pondweeds grown so straight and tall, often three or four yards high, in order to place its little, greenish-brown flower-head above the water's surface. We have spent hours looking down into such a submerged forest, dreaming and wondering about the real meaning of such adaptations.

Although the stem is flexible, the somewhat curved, enlarged portion of it just below the flower-head is rigid; it is also more spongy than the lower part of the stem and is thus fitted to float the flower. The flower itself is one of the prettiest sights that nature has to show us through a lens. It is a Maltese cross, the four reddish stigmas arranged in a solid square at the center; at each side of this central square is a double-barrelled anther, and outside of each anther is a queer, little, dipper-shaped, green sepal. When the anthers open, they push away from the stigmas and throw their pollen toward the outside.

There may be thirty or more of these tiny, cross-shaped flowers in one flower-head. In the bud, the cup-shaped sepals shut down closely, exposing the stigmas first, which would indicate that they ripen before the pollen is shed. The pollen is white, and is floated from plant to plant on the surface of the water; often the water for yards will be covered with this living dust.

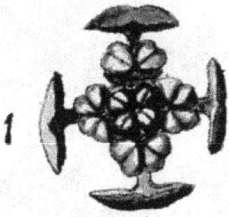

1, Flower of a pondweed enlarged, early stage. 2, Same at later stage.

LESSON

Leading thought— The pondweed lives entirely below the water; at blossom time, however, it sends up its flower stems to the surface of the water, and there sheds its pollen, thus securing cross-pollination.

Method— As this is primarily a lesson that relates to geography, the pondweed should be studied where it is growing. It may be studied in the spring or fall, and the pupils asked to observe the blossoming which occurs in late July. After the pupils have seen where it grows, the plants themselves may be studied in an aquarium, or by placing them in a pail or basin of water. There are confusing numbers of pondweeds but any of them will do for this lesson. The one described in the Teacher's Story is probably *P. perfoliatus.*

Observations—

1. Where is the pondweed found? Does it ever grow out of water? Does it ever grow in very deep water? Does it ever grow in swiftly flowing water?

2. Has the pondweed a root? Does the pondweed need to have water carried to its leaves, as it would if it were living in the air? What is one of the chief uses of the roots to the pondweed? Break off a plant, does it float? Do you think it would float off and die, if it was not anchored by its root?

3. Compare the stem of pondweed with that of any land plant standing straight. What is the chief difference? Why does the pond-

Pond weeds come to the surface when its time to flower

weed not need a stiff stem to hold it up? Cut the stem across, and see if you can observe why it floats.

4. Examine the leaves. Are all of them below the surface of the water? If some float, how do they differ in texture and form from those submerged? How are they arranged on the stem? Are they set close together? What is the difference in texture between its leaves and those of the jewelweed, dock or any other land plant? If any leaves project out of the water are they different in form and texture from those submerged? Sketch the leaf, showing its shape, its edges, and the way it joins the stem.

5. How far below the surface of the water does the pondweed usually lie? Does it ever rise up to the water's surface? When? Have you ever noticed the pondweed in blossom? How does the blossom look on the water? Can you see the white pollen floating on the surface of the water? Look down into the water and see the way the pondweed stands in order to float its blossoms.

6. Study the blossom. Note the stem that bears it. Is the part that bears the flower enlarged and stiffer than the stem below? Do you

think that this enlarged part of the stem acts like the bob on a fish-line? Examine a flower cluster with a lens. How many flowers upon it? Study one flower carefully. Describe the four stigmas at the center. Describe the anthers arranged around them. Describe the sepal which protects each anther. When the anthers open do they discharge the pollen toward or away from the stigmas?

7. What happens after the flowers are pollenated? Do they still float? What sort of seed-capsule has the pondweed? Do the seeds break away and float?

> "Again the wild cow-lily floats
> Her golden-freighted, tented boats,
>   In thy cool caves of softened gloom,
> O'ershadowed by the whispering reed,
> And purple plumes of pickerel weed,
>   And meadow-sweet in tangled bloom.
>
> "The startled minnows dart in flocks,
> Beneath thy glimmering amber rocks,
>   If but a zephyr stirs the brake;
> The silent swallow swoops, a flash
> Of light, and leaves with dainty plash,
>   A ring of ripples in her wake."
>   —"BIRCH STREAM," ANNA BOYNTON AVERILL.

The Cat-Tail

IN June and early July, if the cat-tail be closely observed, it will be seen to have the upper half of the cat's tail much narrower and different in shape from the lower half—as if it were covered with a quite different fur. It seems to be clothed with a fine drooping fringe of olive-yellow. With the aid of a lens, we can see that this fringe is a mass of crowded anthers, two or three of them being attached to the same stalk by a short filament. These anthers are packed full of pollen, which is sifted down upon the pistillate flowers below by every breeze; and with every puff of stronger wind, the pollen is showered over all neighboring flowers to the leeward. There is not much use in trying to find the pistillate flowers in the plush of the cat-tail. They have no sepals nor petals, and are so imbedded in the thick pappus which forms the plush that the search is hardly worth while for nature-study, unless a microscope is used. The ovary is rather long, the style slender, and the stigma reaches out to the cut-plush surface of the cat-tail. The pupils can find what these flowers are by studying the seed; in fact,

A hummingbird collects cattail seed and ballons to line its nest

the seed does not differ very much from the flower, except that it is mature and is browner in color.

It is an interesting process to take apart a cat-tail plant; the lower, shorter leaves surround the base of the plant, giving it size and strength. All the leaves have the same general shape, but vary in length. Each leaf consists of the free portion, which is long and narrow and flat towards its tapering tip but is bent into a trough as it nears the plant, and the lower portion of the leaf, which clasps the plant entirely or partially, depending upon whether it is an outer or inner leaf, and thus adds to its strength. We almost feel as if these alternate leaves were consciously doing their best to protect the slender, flower stem. The free part of the leaves is strengthened by lengthwise veins, and they form edges that never tear nor break. They are very flexible, and therefore yield to the wind rather than defy it. If we look at a leaf in cross-section, we can see the two thick walls strengthened by the framework of stiff veins which divide the interior into long cells. If we cut the leaf lengthwise we can see that these long cells are supported by stiff, coarse partitions.

Where the leaf clasps the stem, it is very stiff and will break rather than bend. The texture of the leaf is soft and smooth, and its shade of green is attractive. The length of the leaves is often greater than that of the blossom stalk, and their graceful curves contrast pleasantly with its ramrod-like stiffness. It is no wonder that artists and the decorators have used the cat-tail lavishly as a model. It is interesting to note that the only portion of the leaves injured by the wind is the extreme tip.

The cat-tail is adapted for living in swamps where the soil is wet but not under water all the time. When the land is drained, or when it is flooded for a considerable time, the cat-tails die out and disappear. They usually occur in marshy zones along lakes or streams; and such

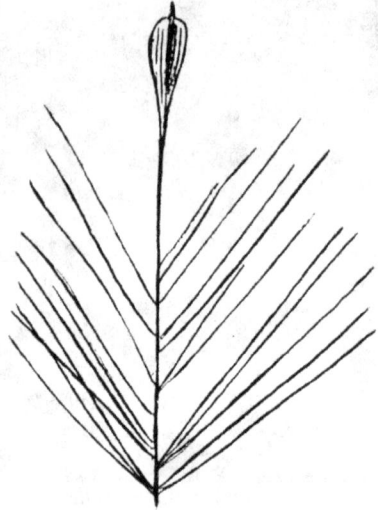

A cattail fruit with its balloon

a zone is always sharply defined by dry land on one side and water on the other. The cat-tail roots are fine and fibrous and are especially fitted, like the roots of the tamarack, to thread the mud of marshy ground and thus gain a foothold. The cat-tails form one of the cohorts in the phalanx of encroaching plants, like the reeds and rushes, which surround and, by a slow march of years, finally conquer and dry up ponds. But in this they overdo the matter, since after a time the soil becomes too dry for them and they disappear, giving place to other plants which find there a congenial environment. The place where I studied the cat-tails as a child is now a garden of joe pye weed and wild sunflowers.

Reference— Plant Life, Coulter.

LESSON

Leading thought— The cat-tail is adapted to places where the soil is wet but not under water; its pollen is scattered by the wind, and its seeds are scattered by wind and water. Its leaves and stalks are not injured nor broken by the wind.

Method—As this is primarily a geography lesson, it should be given in the field if possible; otherwise the pupils must explore for them-

Cattail in blossom. The staminate flower are massed at the tip, and the pistillate flowers which form the "cattail" are massed lower on the stalk

selves to discover the facts. The plant itself can be brought into the schoolroom for study. When studying the seeds, it is well to be careful, or the schoolroom and the pupils will be clothed with the pappus for weeks.

Observations—

1. Where are the cat-tails found? Is the land on which they grow under water all the year? At any part of the year? Is it dry land all the year? What happens to the cat-tails, if the land on which they grow is flooded for a season? What happens to them, if the land is drained?

2. How wide a strip do the cat-tails cover, where you have found them? Are they near a pond or brook or stream? Do they grow out in the stream? Why do they not extend further inland? What is the character of the soil on which they grow?

3. What sort of a root has the cat-tail? Why is this root especially adapted to the soil where cat-tails grow? Describe the rootstock.

4. *The cat-tail plant* . Are the leaves arranged opposite or alternate? Tear off a few of the leaves and describe the difference between the lower and the upper end of a leaf as follows: How do they differ in shape? Texture? Pliability? Color? Width? Does each leaf completely

encircle the stalk at its base? Of what use is this to the plant? Of what use is it to have the plant stiffer where the leaves clasp the stalk? What would happen in a wind storm if this top-heavy, slender seed stalk was bare and not supported by the leaves? What is the special enemy of long, tall, slender-leafed plants?

5. Take a single leaf, cut it across near where it joins the main stalk and also near its tip. Look at the cross-section and see how the leaf is veined. What do its long veins or ribs do for the leaf? Split the leaf lengthwise and see what other supports it has. Does the cat-tail leaf break or tear along its edges easily? Does the wind injure any part of the leaf?

6. Study the cat-tail flowers the last half of June. Note the part that will develop into the cat's tail. Describe the part above it. Can you see where the pollen comes from? The pistillate flowers which are in the plush of the cat-tail have no sepals, petals, odor nor nectar. Do you think that their pollen is carried to them by the bees? How is it carried?

7. Examine the cat-tail in fall or winter. What has happened to that part of the stalk above the cat-tail where the anthers grew? Study two or three of the seeds, and see how they are provided for traveling. What scatters them? Will the cat-tail seed balloons float? Would the wind or the water be more likely to carry the cat-tail seeds to a place where they would grow? Describe the difference between the cat-tail balloon and the thistle balloon.

8. How crowded do the cat-tail plants grow? How are they arranged to keep from shading each other? In how many ways is the wind a friend of the cat-tails?

9. How do the cat-tails help to build up land and make narrower ponds and streams?

Daisies and grasses in a field

A Type Lesson for a Composite Flower

Leading thought— Many plants have their flowers set close together to make a mass of color, like the geraniums or the clovers. But there are other plants where the flowers of one flower-head act like the members of a family, those at the center doing a certain kind of work for the production of seed, and those around the edges doing another kind of work. The sunflower, goldenrod, asters, daisies, cone-flower, thistle, dandelion, burdock, everlasting, and many other common flowers have their blossoms arranged in this way. Before any of the wild-flower members of this family are studied, the lesson on the garden sunflower should be given. (See Sunflowers Lesson in the volume featuring Garden Flowers and Trees page 57).

Method— These flowers may be studied in the schoolroom with suggestions for field observations. A lens is almost necessary for the study of most of these flowers.

Observations—

1. Can you see that what you call the flower consists of many flowers set together like a beautiful mosaic? Those at the center are called disk-flowers; those around the edges banner or ray-flowers.

2. Note that the flowers around the edges have differently shaped corollas than those at the center. How do they differ? Why should these be called the banner flowers? Why should they be called the ray-flowers? How many banner-flowers are there in the flower family you are studying? How are the banners arranged to make the flower-head more attractive? Cut off or pull out all the banner-flowers and see how the flower-head looks. What do the banner-flowers hold out their ban-

ners for? Is it to attract us or the insects? Has the banner-flower any stigma or stamens?

3. Study the flowers at the center. Are they open, or are they unfolded, buds? Can you make a sketch of how they are arranged? Are any of the florets open? What is the shape and the color of the corolla? Can you see the stamen-tubes pushing out from some? What color are the stamen-tubes? Can you see the two-parted stigmas in others? What color is the pollen? Do the florets at the center or at the outside of the disk open first? When they first open, do you see the stamen-tube or the stigma?

4. The flower-heads are protected before they open with overlapping bracts, which may be compared to a shingled house protecting the flower family. As the flower-head opens, these bracts are pushed back beneath it. Describe the shape of these bracts. Are they set in regular, overlapping rows? Are they rough or smooth? Do they end bluntly, with a short point, with a long point, with a spine, or a hook? How do the bracts act when the flower family goes to sleep? Do they remain after the seeds are ripened?

5. Take a flower-head apart, and examine the florets. Can you see what part of the floret will be the seed? Is there a fringe of pappus above it? If so, what will this be on the seed?

6. Study the ripe seeds. How are they scattered? Do they have balloons? Is the balloon close to the seed? Is it fastened to all parts of it?

The Goldenrod

TEACHER'S STORY

ONCE I was called upon to take some children into the field to study autumn flowers. The day we studied goldenrod, I told them the following story on the way, and I found that they were pleased with the fancy and through it were led to see the true purpose of the goldenrod blossoming:

"There are flowers which live in villages and cities, but people who also live in villages and cities are so stupid that they hardly know a flower city when they see it. This morning we are going to visit a golden city where the people are all dressed in yellow, and where they live together in families; and the families all live on top of their little, green, shingled houses, which are set in even rows along the street. In each of these families, there are some flowers whose business it is to furnish nectar and pollen and to produce seeds which have fuzzy balloons; while there are other flowers in each family which wave yellow banners to all the insects that pass by and signal them with a code of their own, thus: 'Here, right this way is a flower family that needs

101

a bee or a beetle or an insect of some sort to bring it pollen from abroad, so that it can ripen its seed; and it will give nectar and plenty of pollen in exchange.' Of course, if the flowers could walk around like people, or fly like insects, they could fetch and carry their own pollen, but as it is, they have to depend upon insect messengers to do this for them. Let us see who of us will be the first to guess what the name of this golden city is, and who will be the first to find it."

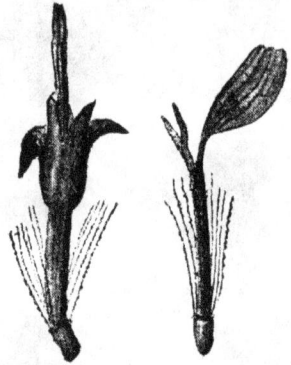

Disc flower and ray flower of goldenrod

The children were delighted with this riddle and soon found the goldenrod city. We examined each little house with its ornate, green "shingles." These little houses, looking like cups, were arranged on the street stem, right side up, in an orderly manner and very close together; and where each joined the stem, there was a little, green bract for a doorstep. Living on these houses we found the flower families, each consisting of a few tubular disk-flowers opening out like bells, and coming from their centers were the long pollen-tubes or the yellow, two-parted stigmas. The ray-flowers had short but brilliant banners; and they, as well as the disk-flowers, had young seeds with pretty fringed pappus developing upon them. The banner-flowers were not set so regularly around the edges as in the asters; but the families were such close neighbors, that the banners reached from one house to another. And all of the families on all of the little, green streets were signalling insects, and one boy said, "They must be making a very loud yellow noise." We found that very many insects had responded to this call—honeybees, bumblebees, mining and carpenter bees, blue-black blister beetles with short wings and awkward bodies, beautiful golden-green chalcid flies, soldier beetles and many others; and we found the spherical gall and the spindle-shaped gall in the stems, and the strange gall up near the top which grew among the leaves.

Unless one is a trained botanist it is wasted energy to try to distinguish any but the well-marked species of goldenrod; for, according to Gray, we have 56 species, the account of which makes twelve pages of

Bees on a goldenrod flower

most uninteresting reading in the new Manual. The goldenrod family is not in the least cliquish, the species have a habit of interbreeding to the confusion of the systematic botanist. Mathew's Field Book serves as well as any for distinguishing the well-marked species.

LESSON

Leading thought— In the goldenrod the flower-heads or families are so small that, in order to attract the attention of the insects, they are set closely together along the stem to produce a mass of color.

Method— Bring to the school-room any kind of goldenrod, and give the lesson on the flowers there. This should be followed by a field excursion to get as many kinds of goldenrod as possible. The following observations will bring out differences in well-marked species:

Observations—

1. Use the Lesson on page 99 to study the flower. How many banner-flowers in the family? How many disk-flowers? Are the banners arranged as regularly around the edges as in the asters and daisies? How are the flower-heads set upon the stems? Which flower-heads open first—those at the base or at the tip of the stem? Do the upper stems of the plant blossom before those lower down?

2. Do the stems bearing flowers come from the axils of the leaves? What is the general shape of the flower branches? Do they come off

evenly at each side, or more at one side? Are the flower branches long or short? Make a sketch of the general shape of the goldenrod you are studying.

3. Is the stem smooth, downy, or covered with bloom? What is its color? In cross-section, is it circular or angular?

4. What is the shape and form of the edges of the lower leaves? The upper ones? Are they set with, or without, petioles on the stem? Do they have a heart-shaped base? Are the leaves smooth or downy? Are they light, or dark green?

5. *Field notes* . Where do you find the goldenrod growing? Do you find one kind growing alone or several kinds growing together? Do you find any growing in the woods? If so, how do they differ in shape from those in the field?

6. How many kinds of insects do you find visiting goldenrod flowers? How many kinds of galls do you find on the goldenrod stems and leaves?

7. Study the goldenrods in November. Describe their seeds and how they are scattered.

> "I am alone with nature,
> With the soft September day;
> The lifting hills above me,
> With goldenrod are gay.
> Across the fields of ether
> Flit butterflies at play;
> And cones of garnet sumac
> Glow down the country way.
> "The autumn dandelion
> Beside the roadway burns;
> Above the lichened boulders
> Quiver the plumèd ferns.
> The cream-white silk of the milkweed
> Floats from its sea-green pod;
> From out the mossy rock-seams
> Flashes the goldenrod."
>
> —MARY CLEMMER AMES.

The Asters

TEACHER'S STORY

L ET us believe that the scientist who gave to the asters their Latin name was inspired. Aster means *star* and these, of all flowers, are most starlike; and in beautiful constellations they border our fields and woodsides. The aster combination of colors is often exquisite. Many have the rays or banners lavender, oar-shaped and set like the rays of a star around the yellow disk-flowers; these latter send out long, yellow anther tubes, overflowing with yellow pollen, and add to the stellar appearance of the flower-head.

"And asters by the brookside make asters in the brook."

Thus sang H. H. of these beautiful masses of autumn flowers. But if H. H. had attempted to distinguish the species, she would have said rather that asters by the brookside make more asters in the book; for Gray's Manual assures us that we have 77 species including widely dif-

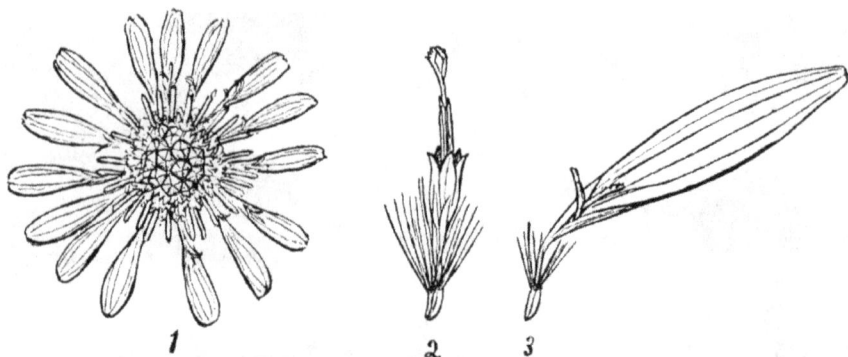

1. an aster flower-head enlarged; 2. a disk-flower; 3. a banner-flower.

ferent forms, varying in size, color and also as to the environment in which they will grow. They range from the shiftless woodland species, which has a few whitish ray-flowers hanging shabbily about its yellow disk and with great, coarse leaves on long, gawky petioles climbing the zigzag stem, to the beautiful and dignified New England aster, which brings the glorious purple and orange of its great flower-heads to decorate our hills in September and October.

Luckily, there are a few species which are fairly well marked, and still more luckily, it is not of any consequence whether we know the species or not, so far as our enjoyment of the flowers themselves is concerned. The outline of this lesson will call the attention of the pupils to the chief points of difference and likeness in the aster species, and they will thus learn to discriminate in a general way. The asters, like the goldenrods, begin to bloom at the tip of the branches, the flower-heads nearest the central stem, blooming last. All of the asters are very sensitive, and the flower-heads will close promptly as soon as they are gathered. The ray or banner-flowers are pistillate, and therefore develop seed. The seed has attached to its rim a ring of pappus, and is ballooned to its final destination. In November, the matured flower-heads are fuzzy, with seeds ready for invitations from any passing wind to fly whither it listeth.

LESSON

Leading thought— There are very many different kinds of asters, and they all have their flowers arranged similarly to those of the sunflower.

Method— Have the pupils collect as many kinds of asters as possible, being careful to get the basal leaves and to take notes on where each kind was found—that is, whether in the woodlands, by the brooksides or in the open fields. This lesson should follow that on the sunflower.

Observations—

1. What was the character of the soil and surroundings where this aster grew? Were there large numbers of this kind growing together? Were the flowers wide open when you gathered them? How soon did they close?

2. How high did the plants stand when growing? Were there many flowers, or few, on each plant?

3. Study the lower and the upper leaves. Describe each as follows: the shape, the size, the edges, the way it was joined to the stem.

4. Is the stem many-branched or few? Do the branches bearing flowers extend in all directions? Are the stems hairy or smooth, and what is their color?

5. What is the diameter of the single flower-head? What is the color of the ray-flowers? How many ray or banner-flowers are there? What is the shape of a single banner as compared with that of a sunflower? What are the colors of the disk-flowers? Of the pollen? Do the disk-flowers change color after blossoming?

6. Look at the bracts below the flower-head. Are they all the same shape? What is their color? Do they have recurved tips or do they overlap closely? Are they sticky?

7. Take the aster flower-head apart and look at it with a lens. In a disk-flower, note the young seed, the pappus, the tubular five-parted corolla, the anther tube and the stigmas. In the ray-flower, find the young seed, the pappus and the stigma.

8. Watch the bees working on asters, and find where they thrust their tongues to reach the nectar.

9. Study an aster plant in November, and describe the seeds and how they are scattered.

Gland bearing jewelweed

The Jewelweed, or Touch-me-not

"Cup bearer to the summer, this floral Hebe shy
Is loitering by the brookside as the season passes by;
And she's strung her golden ewers with spots of brown all flecked,
O'er dainty emerald garments, like a queen with gems bedecked.

She brooks not condescension from mortal hand, you know,
For, touch her e'er so gently, impatiently she'll throw
Her tiny little jewels, concealed in pockets small
Of her dainty, graceful garment, and o'er the ground
they fall."

—Ray Laurence

JEWELS for the asking at the brookside, pendant jewels of pale-gold or red-gold and of strange design! And the pale and the red are different in design, although of the same general pattern. The pale ones seem more simple and open, and we may study them first. If the flowers of the jewelweed have been likened to ladies' earrings, then the bud must be likened to the old-fashioned ear-bob; for it is done up in the neatest little triangular knob imaginable, with a little

108

curly pig-tail appendage at one side, and protected above by two cup-shaped sepals, their pale green seeming like enamel on the pale gold of the bud. It is worth while to give a glance at the stem from which this jewel hangs; it is so delicate and so gracefully curved; and just above the twin sepals is a tiny green bract, elongate, and following the curve of the stem as if it were just a last artistic touch; and though the flowers fall, this little bract remains to keep guard above the seed-pod.

It would take a Yankee, very good at guessing, to make out the parts of this flower, so strange are they in form. We had best begin by looking at the blossom from the back side. The two little, greenish sepals are lifted back like butterfly wings, and we may guess from their position that there are two more sepals, making four in all. These latter are yellow; one is notched at the tip and is lifted above the flower; the other is below and is made into a wide-mouthed triangular sac, ending in a quirl at the bottom, which, if we test it, we shall find is the nectary, very full of sweetness. Now, if we look the flower in the face, perhaps we can find the petals; there are two of them "holding arms" around the mouth of the nectar-sac. And stiff arms they are too, two on a side, for each petal is two-lobed, the front lobe being very short and the posterior lobe widening out below into a long frill, very convenient for the bee to cling to, if she has learned the trick, when prospecting the nectar-sac behind for its treasure. The way this treasure-sac swings backward from its point of attachment above when the insect is probing it, must make the lady bee feel that the joys of life are elusive. Meanwhile, what is the knob projecting down above the entrance to the nectar-sac, as if it were a chandelier in a vestibule? If we look at it with a lens, we can see that it is made up of five chubby anthers, two in front, one at each side and one behind; their short, stout little filaments are crooked just right to bring the anthers together like five closed fingers holding a fist full of pollen-dust, just ready to sift it on the first one that chances to pass below. Thus it is that Madame Bumblebee, who dearly loves the nectar from these flowers, gets her back well dusted with the creamy-white pollen and does a great business for the jewelweed in transferring it. But after the pollen is shed, some day the bumblebee pushes up too hard against the anthers and they break loose, all in a bunch, looking like a crooked legged table; and there in their stead, thus left bare and ready for pollen, is the long green pistil with its pointed stigma ready to rake the pollen out of the fur of any bumblebee that calls.

The red-gold jewelweed is quite different in shape from the pale species. The sepal-sac is not nearly so flaring at the mouth, and the nectar-spur is half as long as the sac and curves and curls under in a most secretive fashion. The shape of the nectar-spur suggests that it was meant for an insect with a long, flexible sucking tube that could curl around and probe it to the bottom; and some butterflies do avail themselves of the contents of this bronze pitcher. Mr. Mathews mentions the *Papilio troilus*, and I have seen the yellow roadside butterfly partaking of the nectar. Professor Robertson believes that the form of the nectar-spur is especially adapted for the hummingbird. But I am sure that the flowers which I have had under observation are the special partners of a small species of bumblebee, which visits these flowers with avidity, celerity, and certainty, plunging into the nectar-sac "like a shot," and out again and in again so rapidly that the eye can hardly follow. One day, one of them accommodatingly alighted on a leaf near me, while she combed from her fur a creamy-white mass of pollen, which matched in color the fuzz on her back, heaping it on her leg baskets. She seemed to know that the pollen was on her back, and it was comical to see her contortions to get it off. The action of these bumblebees in these flowers is in marked contrast to those of the large bumblebees and the honey-bees. One medium-sized species of bumblebee has learned the trick of embracing with the front legs the narrow, stiff portion of the petals which encircles the opening to the sac, thus holding the flower firm while thrusting the head into the sac. While the huge species—black with very yellow plush—does not attempt to get the nectar in a legitimate manner, but systematically alights, back downward, below the sac of the flower, with head toward the curved spur, and cuts open the sac for the nectar. A nectar-robber of the most pronounced type! The honey-bees, Italian hybrids, are the most awkward in their attempts to get nectar from these flowers; they attempt to alight on the expanded portion of the petals and almost invariably slide off between the two petals. They then circle around and take observations with a note of determination in their buzzing, and finally succeed, as a rule, in gaining a foothold and securing the nectar. But the midget bumblebees show a *savoir faire* in probing the orange

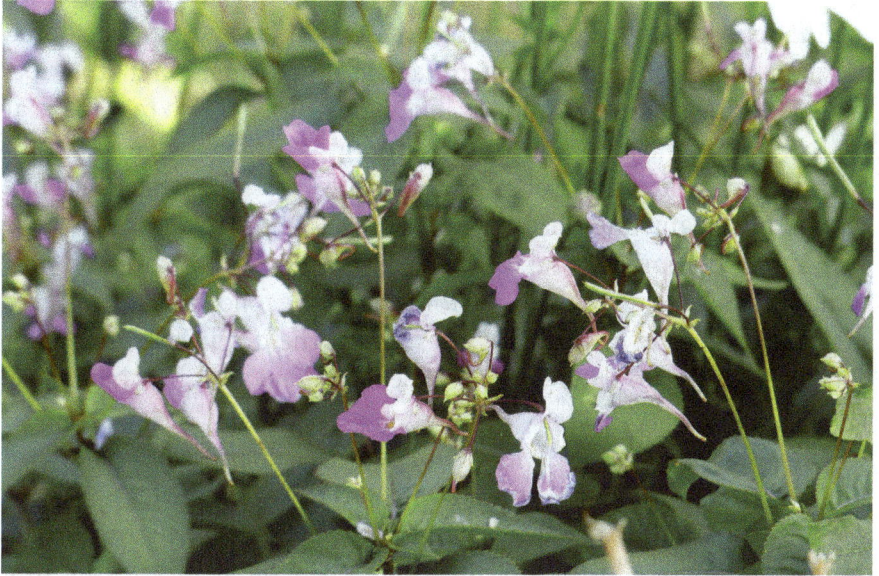
Balfour jewelweed

jewelweed that is convincing; they are so small that they are quite out of sight when in the nectar-sacs.

The jewelweed flowers of the pale species and the pale flowers of the orange species—for this latter has sometimes pale yellow flowers—are not invariably marked with freckles in the nectar-sac. But the most common forms are thus speckled. There is something particularly seductive to insects in these brownish or reddish flecks, and wherever we find them in flowers, we may with some confidence watch for the insects they were meant to allure. The orange jewelweed flower is a model for an artist in its strange, graceful form and its color combination of yellow spotted and marbled with red.

Gray's Manual states that in the jewelweeds are often flowers of two sorts: "The large ones which seldom ripen seeds, and very small ones which are fertilized early in the bud, their floral envelopes never expanding but forced off by the growing pod and carried upward on its apex." My jewelweed patch has not given me the pleasure of observing these two kinds of flowers; my plants blossom luxuriously and profusely, and a large proportion of the flowers develop seed. The little, straight, elongated seed-pods are striped prettily and become quite plump from the large seeds within them. Impatiens? We should say so! This pod which looks so smug and straight-laced that we should never suspect it of being so touchy, at the slightest jar when it is ripe, splits lengthwise into five ribbon-like parts, all of which tear loose at the lower end and fly up in spirals around what was once the tip of the pod, but which now looks like a crazy little turbine wheel with five arms. And meanwhile, through this act the fat, wrinkled seeds have been flung, perhaps several feet away from the parent plant, and presumably to some congenial place for growth the following spring. This surprising method of throwing its seeds is the origin of the popular name touch-me-not, and the scientific name *Impatiens* by which these plants are known.

The jewelweed has other names—celandine and silver-leaf, and ladies' ear-drop. It is an annual with a slight and surface-spreading growth of roots, seeming scarcely strong enough to anchor the branching stems, did not the plants have the habit of growing in a community, each helping to support its neighbor. The stem is round, hollow and much swollen at the joints; it is translucent, filled with moisture, and its outer covering is a smooth silken skin, which may be readily stripped off. Both species of jewelweed vary in the color of their stems, some being green, others red and some dark purple; and all the differing colors may be found within a few yards of each other.

The leaves are alternate, dark green above and a lighter shade below, ovate in form with scalloped edges, with midrib and veins very prominent beneath and depressed on the upper side; they are smooth on both sides to the unaided eye, but with a lens a film of fine, short hairs may be seen, particularly on the under side. When plunged beneath clear water, they immediately take on the appearance of burnished silver; when removed, no drop remains on their surface.

The flower stems spring from the axils of the leaves and are very slender and thread-like, and the flowers nod and swing with every breeze. They grow in open, drooping clusters, few blossoms open at a time, and with buds and seed-capsules present in various stages of growth.

The jewelweed is involuntarily most hospitable, and always houses many uninvited guests, as well as the bee-callers which are invited. Galls are formed on the leaves and flowers; the hollow stems are in-

Orange jewelweed

habited by stalk-borers; leaf-miners live between the upper and under surfaces of the leaves, making curious arabesque patterns and initials as if embroidering milady's green gown.

LESSON

Leading thought— The jewelweed may be found by the brookside, in swamps, or in any damp and well-shaded area. It is provided with a remarkable contrivance for scattering its seeds far afield. It has no liking for open sunny places, unless very damp. There are two kinds, often found growing together, though the spotted touch-me-not (*Impatiens biflora*) is said to be more widely distributed than its relative— the golden, or pale, touch-me-not (*Impatiens aurea*).

Method— The jewelweeds should be studied where they are growing; but if this is impracticable, a large bouquet of both kinds (if possible), bearing buds, blossoms, and seed-capsules, and one or two plants with roots, may be brought to the schoolroom.

In the fields the children may see how well the plant is provided with means to sustain itself in its chosen ground, and thus lead them to look with keener eyes at other common weeds.

Observations—

1. Do you think the jewelweed is an annual, sustaining life in its seeds during winter, or do its roots survive?

2. Do the roots strike deeply into the soil, or spread near the surface?

3. Study the stem; is it hard and woody or juicy and translucent, rough or smooth, solid or hollow?

4. Note the shape and position of the leaves; do they grow opposite or alternately on the stalk? Are their edges entire, toothed or scalloped? Do they vary in color on upper and lower surface? Are they smooth or in the least degree rough or hairy? Plunge a plant under clear water in a good light and observe the beautiful transformation. Does the water cling to the leaves?

5. Where do the flower-stems spring from the main stalk? Do the flowers grow singly or in clusters? Do the blossoms all open at nearly the same time or form a succession of bud, flower and seed on the same stem?

6. Study the parts of the flower. Find the four sepals and describe the shape and position of each. Describe the nectar-sac in the nectar-horn. Can you find the two petals? Can you see that each petal has a lobe near where it joins the stem? Find the little knob hanging down above the entrance of the nectar-sac; of what is it composed? Look at it with a lens, and tell how many stamens unite to make the knob. Where is the pollen and what is its color? What insect do you think could reach the nectar at the bottom of the spurred sac? Could any insect get at the nectar without rubbing its back against the flat surface of the pollen boxes? What remains after the stamens fall off? Describe how the bees do the work of pollenation of the jewelweeds. Write or tell as a story your own observations on the actions of the different bees visiting these flowers.

7. Carefully observe a seed-capsule without touching it; can you see the lines of separation between its sections? How many are there? What happens when the pod is touched? Are the loosened sections attached at the stem, or at the apex of the pod? Hold a pod at arm's length when discharging its contents and measure the distance to which the seeds are thrown. Of what use is this habit of seed-throwing to the plant?

8. Describe the differences in shape and color between the pale yellow and the orange jewelweeds. Watch to see if the same insects visit both. Which species do you think is best suited to the bumblebees?

Weeds

Chicory enough to make anyone see blue

Weeds

"The worst weed in corn may be—corn."

—PROFESSOR I. P. ROBERTS.

NATURE is the great farmer. Continually she sows and reaps, making all the forces of the universe her tools and helpers; the sun's rays, wind, rain and snow, insects and birds, animals small and great, even to the humble burrowing worms of the earth—all work mightily for her, and a harvest of some kind is absolutely sure. But if man interferes and insists that the crops shall be only such as may benefit and enrich himself, she seems to yield a willing obedience, and under his control does immensely better work than when unguided. But Dame Nature is an "eye-servant." Let the master relax his vigilance for ever so short a time, and among the crops of his desire will come stealing in the hardy, aggressive, and to him, useless plants that seem to be her favorites.

A weed is a plant growing where we wish something else to grow, and a plant may, therefore, be a weed in some locations and not in others. The mullein is grown in greenhouses in England as the Ameri-

117

can velvet-plant. Our grandmothers considered "butter-and-eggs," a pretty posy, and planted it in their gardens, wherefrom it escaped, and is now a bad weed wherever it grows. A weed may crowd out our cultivated plants, by stealing the moisture and nourishment in the soil which they should have; or it may shade them out by putting out broad leaves and shutting off their sunlight. When harvested with a crop, weeds may be unpalatable to the stock which feed upon it; or in some cases, as in the wild parsnip, the plant may be poisonous.

Each weed has its own way of winning in the struggle with our crops, and it behooves us to find that way as soon as possible in order to circumvent it. This we can only do by a careful study of the peculiarities of the species. To do this we must know the plant's life history; whether it is an annual, surviving the winter only in its seeds; or a biennial, storing in fleshy root or in broad, green leafy rosette the food drawn from the soil and air during the first season, to perfect its fruitage in the second year; or a perennial, surviving and springing up to spread its kind and pester the farmer year after year, unless he can destroy it "root and branch." Purslane is an example of the first class, burdock or mullein of the second, and the field sorrel or Canada thistle of the third. According to their nature the farmer must use different means of extermination; he must strive to hinder the annuals and biennials from forming any seed whatever; and where perennials have made themselves a pest, he must put in a "hoed crop," requiring such constant and thorough tillage that the weed roots will be deprived of all starchy food manufactured by green leaves and be starved out. Especially every one who plants a garden should know how the weeds look when young, for seedlings of all kinds are delicate and easy to kill before their roots are well established.

OUTLINE FOR THE STUDY OF A WEED

1. Why do we call a plant a weed? Is a weed a weed wherever it grows? How about "butter and eggs" when it grew in Grandmother's garden? Why do we call that a weed now? What did Grandmother call it?

2. In how many ways may a weed injure our cultivated crops?

3. Why must we study the habits of a weed before we know how to fight it?

We should ask of every weed in our garden or on our land the following questions, and let it answer them through our observations in order to know why the weed grows where it chooses, despite our efforts.

4. How did this weed plant itself where I find it growing? By what agency was its seed brought and dropped?

5. What kind of root has it? If it has a tap-root like the mullein, what advantage does it derive from it? If it has a spreading shallow-growing root like the purslane what advantage does it gain? If it has a creeping rootstock with underground buds like the Canada thistle, how is it thereby helped?

6. Is the stem woody or fleshy? Is it erect or reclining or climbing? Does it gain any advantage through the character of its stem?

7. Note carefully the leaves. Are they eaten by grazing animals? If not, why? Are they covered with prickles like the teasel or fuzz like the mullein, or are they bitter and acrid like the wild carrot?

8. Study the blossoms. How early does the weed bloom? How long does it remain in bloom? Do insects carry pollen for the flowers? If so, what insects? What do the insects get in return? How are the flower buds and the ripening seeds protected?

9. Does it ripen many seeds? Are these ripened at the same time or are they ripened during a long period? Of what advantage is this? How are the seeds scattered, carried and planted? Compute how many seeds one plant of this weed matures in one year.

"That which ye sow ye reap. See yonder fields!
The sesamum was sesamum, the corn
Was corn. The Silence and the Darkness know!"
—EDWIN ARNOLD.

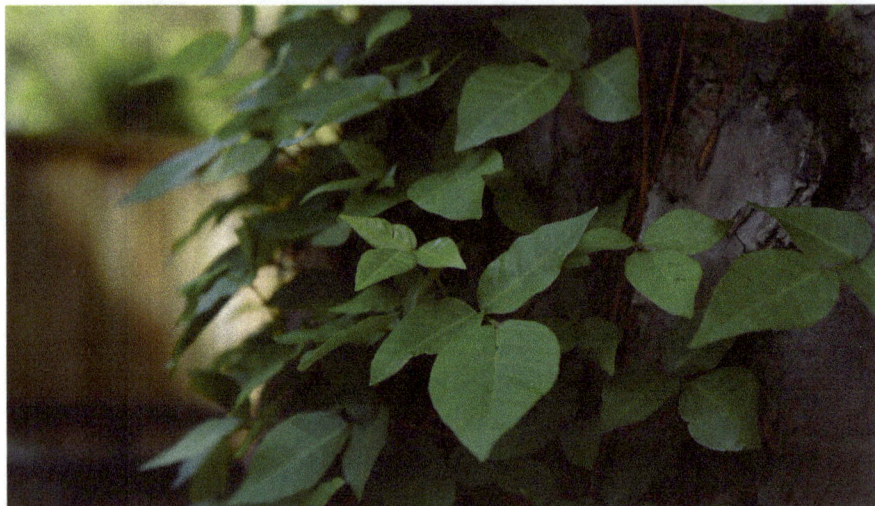

Poison Ivy

Poison ivy may be found creeping over the ground, climbing as a vine, attached by aerial roots to trees, walls, or fences, or growing erect as a shrub. The alternate, compound leaves are made up of three leaflets, and this has given rise to the line often quoted:

Leaflets three, let it be.

During the fall and winter, the plant can usually be identified by the presence of clusters of small, white, berry-like fruits. It is thus easily distinguished from the woodbines or Virginia creepers which have leaves made up of five or more leaflets and in late summer have clusters of blue berries.

PREVENTION OF IVY POISONING AFTER CONTACT WITH THE PLANT

Wash the hands, the face, or affected parts in a solution of 5 per cent iron chloride in a half-and-half mixture of alcohol and water. If this solution is applied before or immediately after going into a region where poison ivy is known to grow no harmful effects need be expected. This remedy is non poisonous and inexpensive and it can be obtained at almost any drug store.

If the iron chloride is not available, considerable protection from

Leaves of poison ivy and poison sumac and some harmless plants with which they are often confused

1. Poison ivy, *Rhus toxicodendron*. Leaf Stalk bearing three leaflets: buds visible. 2, Virginia creeper, *Parthenocissus quinquefolia* Leafstalk bearing five leaflets. 3. Silky dogwood. *Cornus amomum*. Leafstalk with one blade leaves opposite 4. Fragrant sumac, *Rhus canadensis* Leaf Stalk bearing three leaflets buds hidden under base of Leafstalk. 5, Poison sumac, *Rhus vernix*. Leaves alternate: leafstalk bearing several leaflets with smooth margins; buds visible. 6, Dwarf sumac, *Rhus copallina*. Margin of leaflets smooth or toothed leaf axis winged. 7. Smooth sumac, *Rhus glabra*, Margin of leaflet toothed, buds hidden under base of leafstalks. 8. Staghorn sumac, *Rhus Typhina*, Like 7 but leaves and twigs are hairy 9. Mountain ash. *Sorbus americana*. Margin of leaflets toothed buds visible. 10, Black ash. *Fraxinus nigra Marsh*. Leaves and buds opposite. 11, Elderberry, *Sambucus canadensis*. Leaves and buds opposite

the effects of exposure to poison ivy may be secured by thoroughly washing the skin of the affected parts several times with hot water and a laundry soap that contains an excess of free alkali. Use a heavy lather and rinse off at least three or four times.

CURATIVE TREATMENT WHEN POISONING HAS BEGUN

Soaking in hot water usually gives relief. The application of baking soda, one or two teaspoons to a cup of water, is often effective in relieving the pain caused by the inflammation. To soothe the pain and prevent the general spread of the inflammation, fluid extract of Grindelia diluted with six to ten parts of water is recommended. This may be applied with a clean bandage, which should be kept moist and frequently changed.

Do not apply ointment or other oily substances until after the poison has exhausted itself. Sugar of lead is not recommended.

If the case of poisoning is a severe one, it is best to consult a physician before attempting to use any remedy.

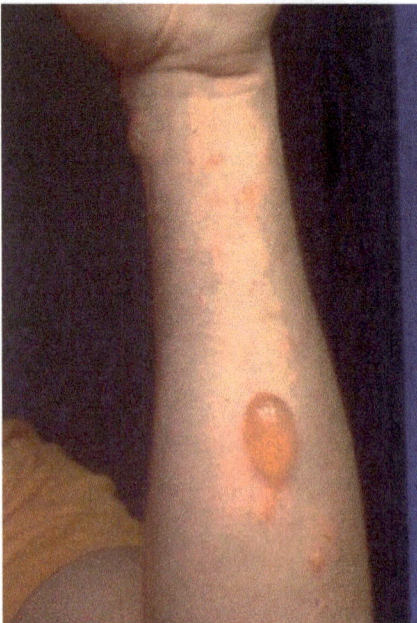

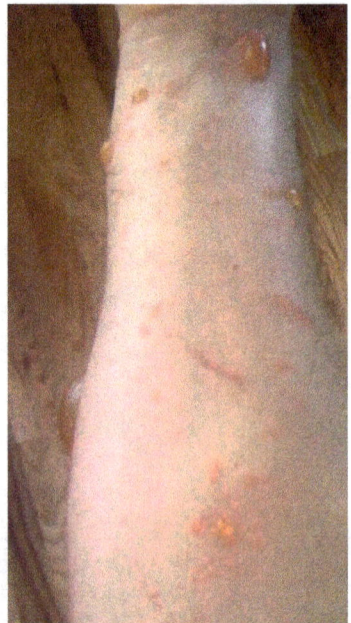

Blisters 72 hours after contact with poison ivy

The Common Buttercup

TEACHER'S STORY

"The buttercups, bright-eyed and bold,
Held up their chalices of gold
To catch the sunshine and the dew."

Buttercups and daisies are always associated in the minds of the children, because they grow in the same fields; yet the two are so widely different in structure that they may reveal to the child something of the marvelous differences between common flowers; for the buttercup is a single flower, while the single daisy is a large family of flowers.

The buttercup sepals are five elongated cups, about one-half as long as the petals; they are pale yellow with brownish tips, but in the globular buds, they are green. The petals are normally five in number, but have a tendency to double, so that often there are six or more; the petals are pale beneath, but on the inside they are most brilliant yellow, and shine as if varnished. Probably it is due to this luminous color that one child is able to determine whether another likes butter or not, by noting when the flower is held beneath the chin, if it makes a yellow reflection; it would be a sodden complexion indeed that would not reflect yellow under this provocation. Each petal is wedge-shaped, and its broad outer edge is curved so as to help make a cuplike flower; if a fallen petal be examined, a tiny scale will be found at its base, as if its point had been folded back a trifle. However, this is not a mere

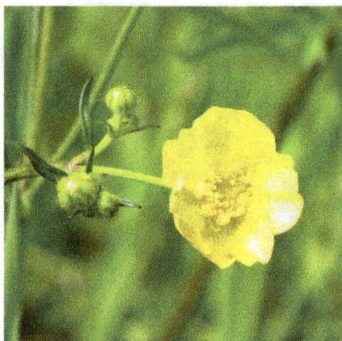

Do you like butter?

fold, but is a little scale growing there—a scale with a mission, for beneath it is developed the nectar.

When the buttercup first opens, all of the anthers are huddled in the center, so that it looks like a golden nest full of golden eggs. Later the filaments stretch up, lifting the anthers into a loose, rounded tuft, almost concealing the bunch of pistils which are packed close together beneath every stigma, like Br'er Rabbit, "laying low." Later, the filaments straighten back, throwing the anthers in a fringy ring about the pale green pistils; and each pistil sends up a short, yellowish stigma. The anthers open away from the pistils and thus prevent self-pollenation to some degree; they also seem to shed much of their pollen before the stigmas are ready to receive it.

Sometimes petals and sepals fall simultaneously and sometimes first one or the other; but they always leave the green bunch of pistils with a ragged fringe of old stamens clinging to them. Later the seeds mature, making a globular head. Each seed is a true akene; it is flattened and has at its upper end a short, recurved hook which may serve to help it to catch a ride on passers-by. However, the seeds are largely scattered by the winds.

The buttercup grows in sunny situations, in fields and along roadsides, but it cannot stand the shade of the woods. It is a pretty plant; its long stems are downy near the bottom, but smooth near the flower; the leaves show a variety of forms on the same plant; the lower ones have many, (often seven) deeply cut divisions, while the upper ones may have three irregular lobes, the middle one being the longest. Beetles are very fond of the nectar and pollen of buttercups, and therefore

Buttercup flower enlarged. Note the scale covering the nectar at the base of the falling petal.

are its chief pollen carriers; but flies and small bees and other insects also find their food in these brilliant colored cups.

LESSON

Leading thought— The buttercup grows with the white daisies, in sunny places, but each buttercup is a single flower, while each daisy is a flower family.

Method— Buttercups brought by the pupils to school may serve for this lesson.

Observations—

1. Look at the back of a flower of the buttercup. What is there peculiar about the sepals? How do the sepals look on the buttercup bud? How do they look later?

2. Look into the flower. How many petals are there? Are there the same number of petals in all the flowers of the same plant? What is the shape of a petal? Compare its upper and lower sides. Take a fallen petal, and look at its pointed base with a lens and note what is there.

3. How do the stamens look? Do you think you can count them? When the flower first opens how are the stamens arranged? How, later? Do the anthers open towards, or away, from the pistils?

4. Note the bunch of pistils at the center of the flower. How do they look when the flower first opens? How, later?

5. When the petals fall, what is left? Can you see now how each little pistil will develop into a seed?

6. Describe the seed-ball and the seed.

7. Look at the buttercup's stems. Are they as smooth near the base as near the flower? Compare the upper leaf with the lower leaf, and note the difference in shape and size.

8. Where do the buttercups grow? Do we find them in the woods? What insects do you find visiting the flowers?

The Hedge Bindweed

I once saw by the roadside a beautiful pyramid, covered completely with green leaves and beset with pink flowers. I stopped to examine this bit of landscape gardening, and for the first time in my life I felt sorry for a burdock; for this burdock had met its match and more in standing up against a weakling plant which it must have scorned at first, had it been capable of this sensation. Its mighty leaves had withered, its flower-stems showed no burs, for the bindweed had caught it in its hundred embraces and had squeezed the life out of it. Once in Northern Florida our eyes were delighted with the most beautiful garden we had ever seen and which resolved itself later into a field of corn, in which every plant had been made a trellis for the bindweed; there it flaunted its pink and white flowers in the sunshine with a grace and charm that suggested nothing of the oppressor.

Sometimes the bindweed fails to find support to lift it into the air. Then it quite as cheerfully mats itself over the grass, making a carpet of exquisite pattern. This vine has quite an efficient way of taking hold. It lifts its growing tips into the air, swaying them joyously with every breeze; and the way each extreme tip is bent into a hook seems

126

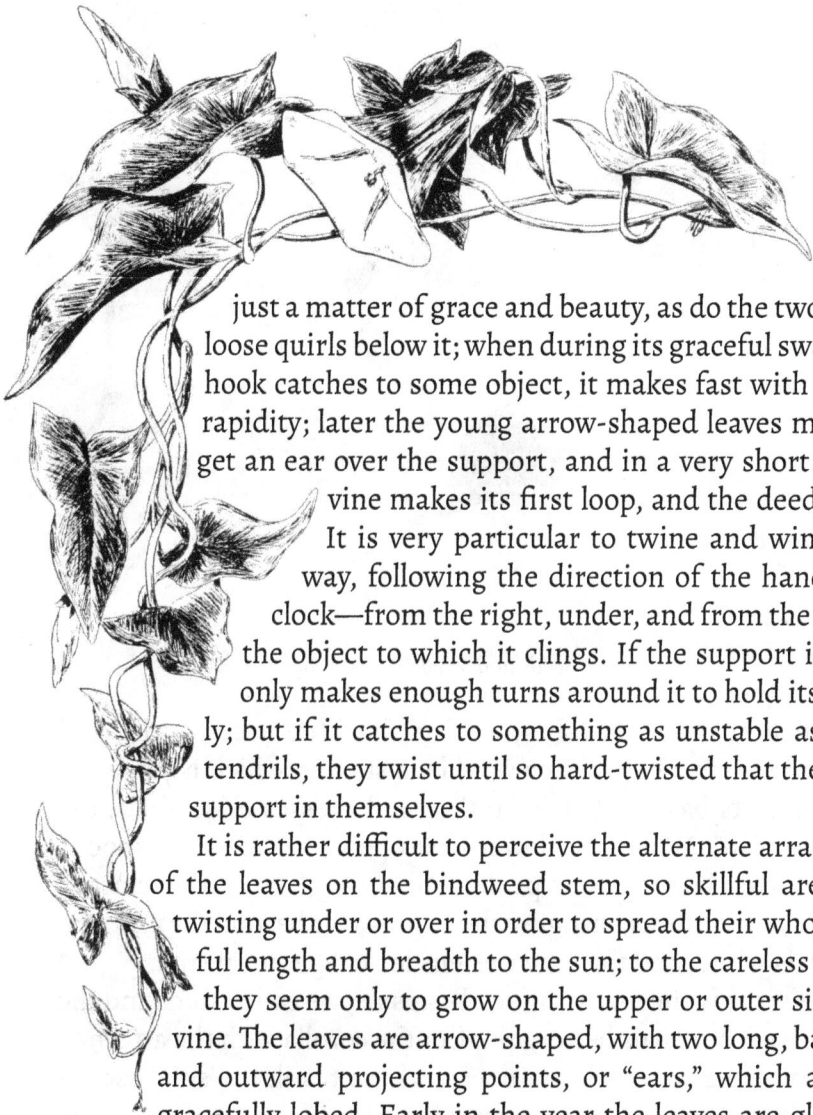

just a matter of grace and beauty, as do the two or three loose quirls below it; when during its graceful swaying the hook catches to some object, it makes fast with amazing rapidity; later the young arrow-shaped leaves manage to get an ear over the support, and in a very short time the vine makes its first loop, and the deed is done. It is very particular to twine and wind in one way, following the direction of the hands of the clock—from the right, under, and from the left, over the object to which it clings. If the support is firm, it only makes enough turns around it to hold itself firmly; but if it catches to something as unstable as its own tendrils, they twist until so hard-twisted that they form a support in themselves.

It is rather difficult to perceive the alternate arrangement of the leaves on the bindweed stem, so skillful are they in twisting under or over in order to spread their whole graceful length and breadth to the sun; to the careless observer they seem only to grow on the upper or outer side of the vine. The leaves are arrow-shaped, with two long, backward, and outward projecting points, or "ears," which are often gracefully lobed. Early in the year the leaves are glossy and perfect; but many insects love to nibble them, so that by September, they are usually riddled with holes.

The flower bud is twisted as if the bindweed were so in the habit of twisting that it carried the matter farther than necessary. Enveloping the base of the flower bud are two large sepal-like bracts, each keeled like a duck's breast down the center; if these are pulled back, it is seen that they are not part of the flower, because they join the stem below it. There are five pale green sepals of unequal sizes, so that some look like fragments of sepals. The corolla is long, bell-shaped, opening with five, starlike lobes; each lobe has a thickened white center; and while its margins are usually pink, they are sometimes a vivid pink-purple and sometimes entirely white. Looking down into this flower-bell, and following the way pointed out by the white star-points which hold out the lobes, we find five little nectar-wells; and each two of these wells are separated by a stamen which is joined to the corolla at its base and at its anther-end presses close about the style of the pistil. When the flower first opens, it shows the spoon-shaped stigmas close together, pushing up through the anther cluster; later, the style elongates, bringing the stigmas far beyond the anthers. The pollen is white, and through the lens looks like tiny pearls.

Seeds and dried pods of hedge bindweed

When we study the maturing seed-capsule, we can understand the uneven size of the sepals better; for after the corolla with the attached stamens falls, the sepals close up around the pistil; the smallest sepal wraps it first, and the larger ones in order of size, enfolding the precious parcel; and outside of all, the great, leafy bracts with their strong keels provide protection. The pod has two cells and two seeds in each cell. But it is not by seeds alone that the bindweed spreads; it is the running rootstock which, when the plant once gets a start, helps it to cover a large area. The bindweed is a relative of the morning-glory and it will prove an interesting study to compare the two in methods of twining, in the time of day of the opening of the flowers, the shape of the leaves, etc. So far as my own observations go, the bindweed flowers seem to remain open only during the middle of the day, but Müller says the flowers stay open on moonlight nights to invite the hawk-moths. This is an interesting question for investigation, and it may be settled by a child old enough to make and record truthful observations.

There are several species of bindweed, but all agree in general habits. The field bindweed lacks the bracts at the base of the flower.

LESSON

Leading thought— There are some plants which have such weak stems that they are obliged to cling to objects for support. The bindweed is one of these, and the way that it takes hold of objects and grows upon them is an interesting story.

Method— It is better to study this plant where it grows; but if this is not practical, the vine with its support should be brought into the schoolroom, the two being carefully kept in their natural relative positions. Several of the questions should be given to the pupils for their personal observation upon this vine in the field. It is an excellent study for pencil or water-color drawing.

Observations—

1. How does the bindweed get support, so that its leaves and its flowers may spread out in the sunshine? Why does its own stem not support it? What would happen to a plant with such a weak stem, if it did not twine upon other objects?

2. How does it climb upon other plants? Does its stem always wind or twist in the same direction? How does it first catch hold of the other plant? If the supporting object is firm, does it wind as often for a given space as when it has a frail support? Can you see the reason for this?

3. Look at the leaves. Sketch one, to be sure that you see its beautiful form and veins. Note if the leaves are arranged alternately on the stem, and then observe how and why they seem to come from one side of the stem. Why do they do this?

4. What is there peculiar about the flower bud? Look at its stem carefully and describe it. Cut it across and look at the end with a lens and describe it. Turn back two sepal-like bracts at the base of the flower or bud. Are they a part of the flower, or are they below it? Find the true sepals. How many are there? Are they all the same size?

Bindweed growing around other plants

5. Examine the flower in blossom. What is its shape? Describe its colors. Look down into it. How many stamens are there, and how are they set in the flower? How does the pistil look when the flower first opens? Later? Can you see the color of the pollen? Can you find where the nectar is borne? How many nectar-wells are there?

6. What insects do you find visiting bindweed flowers? Do the flowers remain open at night or on dark days?

7. Study the seed-capsule. How is it protected on the outside? What next enfolds it? Can you see now the uses of the sepals of several sizes? Cut a seed-capsule across with all its coverings, and see how it is protected. How many seeds are there in the capsule?

8. Has the bindweed other methods of spreading than by seeds? Look at the roots and tell what you observe about them.

9. Make a study of the plant on which the bindweed is climbing, and tell what has happened to it.

10. Compare the bindweed with the morning-glory, and notice the differences and resemblances.

Supplementary reading: "Morning-Glory Stories," in *Flowers and Their Friends*, Morley; *Botany Reader*, Newell, Chap. 10; Golden Numbers, page 74.

STAN SHEBS (CC BY-SA 2.5)

Dodder growing on sage in the Mojave desert

The Dodder

TEACHER'S STORY

If Sinbad's "Old Man of the Sea" had been also a sneak thief, then we might well liken him to dodder. There is an opportunity for an excellent moral lesson connected with the study of dodder and its underhand ways. When a plant ceases to be self-supporting, when it gets its own living from the food made by other plants for their own sustenance, it loses its own power of food-making; and the dodder is an excellent example of the inevitable punishment for "sponging" a living. The dodder has no leaves of its own for it does not need to manufacture food nor to digest it. Its dull yellow stems reach out in long tendrils, swayed by every breeze, until they come in contact with some other plant to which they at once make fast. One of these tendrils seizes its victim plant as a serpent winds its prey, except that it always winds in the same direction—it passes under from the right side and over from the left. Who knows whether the serpents are always so methodical! After dodder gets its hold, little projections appear upon its coiled stems, which look like the prolegs of a caterpillar; but they are not legs, they are suckers, worse than those of the devil-fish; for the latter uses its suckers only to hold fast its prey; but the dodder uses its suckers to penetrate the bark of its victim, and reach down to the sap channels where they may, vampirelike, suck the blood from their victims, or rather the matured sap which is flowing from the leaves to the growing points of the host plant. Not having anything else to do, dodder devotes its energies to the producing of seeds, in order to do more mischief. The species which attack clover and other farm crops seem to manage to get their seeds harvested with the rest; and the farmer who does not know how to test his clover seed for impurities, sows with it the seeds of its enemy.

The dodder flowers are small, globular and crowded together. The calyx has five lobes; the corolla is globular, with five little lobes around its margin and a stamen set in each notch. A few of the species have a four-lobed calyx and corolla; but however many the lobes, the flowers are shiftless looking and are yellowish or greenish white; despite its shiftless appearance, however, each flower manages to mature four perfectly good, plump seeds.

There are, according to Gray, nine species of dodder more or less common in America. Some of the species, among which is the flax dodder, live only upon certain other species of plant life, while others take almost anything that comes within reach. Where it flourishes, it grows so abundantly that it makes large yellow patches in fields, completely choking out the leaves of its victims.

LESSON

Leading thought— There are some plants which not only depend upon other plants to hold them up, but they suck the life-juice from these plants and thus they steal their living.

Method— Bring in dodder with the host plant for the pupils to

Dodder flowers

study in the schoolroom, and ask them to observe afterwards the deadly work of this parasite in the field.

Observations—

1. What is the color of the stem? In which direction does it wind?

2. How is the stem fastened to the host plant? Tear off these suckers and examine the place where they were attached with a lens, and note if they enter into the stem of the host plant.

3. How does the dodder get hold of its victim? Has the dodder any leaves of its own? How can it get along and grow without leaves?

4. How do the flowers look through a lens? Are there many flowers? Can you see the petal lobes and the stamens?

5. How many seeds does each flower develop? How do the seeds look? In what way are they a danger to our agriculture?

I should also avoid the information method. It does a child little good merely to tell him matters of fact. The facts are not central to him and he must retain them by a process of sheer memory; and in order that the teacher may know whether he remembers, the recitation is employed,—re-cite, to tell over again. The educational processes of my younger days were mostly of this order,—the book or the teacher told, I re-told, but the results were always modified by an unpredictable coefficient of evaporation. Good teachers now question the child to discover what he has found out or what he feels, or to suggest what further steps may be taken, and not to mark him on what he remembers. In other words, the present-day process is to set the pupil independently at work, whether he is young or old, and the information-leaflet or lesson does not do this. Of course, it is necessary to give some information, but chiefly for the purpose of putting the pupil in the way of acquiring for himself and to answer his natural inquiries; but information-giving about nature subjects is not nature-study.

—L. H. BAILEY IN "THE OUTLOOK TO NATURE."

The White Daisy

TEACHER'S STORY

EVERY child loves this flower, and yet it is not well understood; it is always at hand for study from June until the frosts have laid waste the fields. However much enjoyment we get from the study of this beautiful flower-head, we should study the plant as a weed also, for it is indeed a pest to those farmers who do not practice a rotation of crops. Its root is long and tenacious of the soil, and it ripens many seeds which mingle with the grass seed, and thus the farmer sows it to his own undoing. The bracts of the involucre, or the shingles of the daisy-house, are rather long, and have parchment like margins. They overlap in two or three rows. In the daisy flower-head, the banner-flowers are white; there may be twenty or thirty of these, making a beautiful frame for the golden-yellow disk-flowers. The banner is rather broad, is veined, and toothed at the tip. The banner-flower has a pistil which shows its two-parted stigma at the base of the banner, and it matures a seed. The disk-flowers are brilliant yellow, tubular, rather short, with the five points of the corolla curling back. The anther-tubes and the

A daisy meadow

pollen are yellow, so are the stigmas. The arrangement of the buds at the center is exceedingly pretty. The flowers develop no pappus, and therefore the seeds have no balloons. They depend upon the ignorance and helplessness of man to scatter their seeds far and wide with the grass and clover seed, which he sows for his own crops. It was thus that it came to America, and in this manner still continues to flaunt its banners in our meadows and pastures. The white daisy is not a daisy, but a chrysanthemum. It has never been called by this name popularly, but has at least twenty other common names, among them the ox-eye daisy, moonpenny, and herb-Margaret.

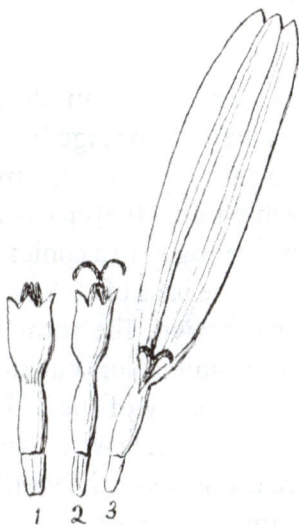

Daisy florets.
1. Disk-flower in pollen-stage; 2. Disk-flower in stigma stage; 3. Ray-flower. All enlarged.

LESSON

Leading thought— The white-daisy is not a single flower but is made up of many little flowers and should be studied by the outline given in the Lesson on page 99.

135

The Yellow Daisy, or Black-Eyed Susan

TEACHER'S STORY

THESE beautiful, showy flowers have rich contrasts in their color scheme. The ten to twenty-ray flowers wave rich, orange banners around the cone of purple-brown disk-flowers. The banners are notched and bent downward at their tips; each banner-flower has a pistil, and develops a seed. The disk-flowers are arranged in a conical, button-like center; the corollas are pink-purple at the base of the tube, but their five recurved, pointed lobes are purple-brown. The anther-tube is purple-brown and the stigmas show the same color; but the pollen is brilliant orange, and adds much to the beauty of the rich, dark florets when it is pushed from the anther-tubes. There is no pappus developed, and the seeds are carried as are the seeds of the white daisy, by being harvested with the seeds of grain.

The stem is strong and erect; the bracts of the involucre, or "shingles," are long, narrow and hairy, the lower ones being longer and wider than those above; they all spread out flat, or recurve below the open flower-head. In blossoming, first the ray-flowers spread wide

their banners; then the flowerets around the base of the cone open and push out their yellow pollen through the brown tubes; then day by day the blossoming circle climbs toward the apex—a beautiful way of blossoming upward.

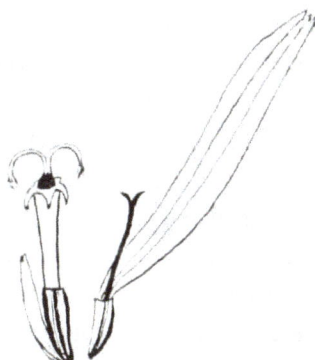

Disk-flower and ray-flower

LESSON

Leading thought— This flower should be studied by the outline given in the Lesson on page 99.

The Thistle

TEACHER'S STORY

N looking at the thistle from its own standpoint, we must acknowledge it to be a beautiful and wonderful plant. It is like a knight of old encased in armor and with lance set, ready for the fray. The most impressive species is the great pasture, or bull, thistle (*C. pumilis*), which has a blossom-head three inches across. This is not so common as the lance-leaved thistle, which ornaments roadsides and fence corners, where it may remain undisturbed for the necessary second year of growth before it can mature its seeds. The most pernicious species, from the farmer's standpoint, is the Canada thistle. Its roots are perennial, and they invade garden, grain field and meadow. They creep for yards in all directions, just deep enough to be sure of moisture, and send up new plants here and there, especially if the main stalk is cut off. Roots severed by the plow, send up shoots from both of the broken parts. Not so with the common thistle, which has a single main root, with many fibrous and clustered branches but with no side shoots.

The stalk of the lance-leaved thistle is strong and woody, and is closely hugged by pricky leaf stems, except for a few inches above the root. The leaves are placed alternately on the stalk; they are deep green, covered above with rough and bristling hairs, and when young are covered on the under side with soft, gray wool which falls away later. The spines grow on the edges of the leaves, which are deeply lobed and are also somewhat wavy and ruffled, thus causing the savage spears to meet the enemy in any direction. The ribs and veins are without spines. Small buds or branches may be found at the axils of the leaves; and if a plant is beheaded, those axiliary buds nearest the top of the stem will grow vigorously.

The thistle flowers are purple in color and very fragrant; they grow in single heads at the summit of the stalk, and from the axils of the upper leaves. The topmost heads open first. Of the individual flowers in the head, those of the outer rows first mature and protrude their pistils; the pollen grains are white. In each flower, the corolla is tube-shaped and purple, parting into five fringelike lobes at the top, and fading to white at its nectar-filled base.

A floret from a thistle flower-head.

The stamens have dark purple anthers, united in a tube in which their pollen is discharged. The pistil, ripening later, shoves out the pollen with its stigma, which at first is blunt at the end, its two-parted lips so tightly held together that not a grain of its own flower's pollen can be taken. But when thrust far out beyond the anther-tube, the two-parted stigma opens to receive the pollen which is brought by the many winged visitors; for of all flowers, the thistles with their abundant nectar are the favorites of insects. Butterflies of many species, moths, beetles and bees—especially the bumblebees—are the happy guests of the thistle blooms.

The thistles believe in large families; a single head of the lance-leaved thistle has been known to have 116 seeds. The seeds are oblong, pointed, little akenes, with hard shells. Very beautiful and wonderful is the pappus of the thistle; it is really the calyx of the flower, its tube being a narrow collar, and the lobes are split up into the silken floss. At the larger end of the seed is a circular depression with a tiny hub at its center; into this ring, and around the knob, is fitted the collar

which attaches the down to the seed. Hold the balloon between the eye and the light, and it is easy to see that the down is made of many-branched plumes which interlace and make it more buoyant. When first taken from its crowded position on the flower-head, the pappus surrounds the corolla in a straight, close tube; but if placed for just a few moments in the sun, the threads spread, the filmy branchlets open out, and a fairy parachute is formed, with the seed hanging beneath; if no breath of air touches it while spreading, it will sometimes form a perfect funnel; when blown upon, some of the silken threads lose their places on the rim and rise to the center. When driven before the breeze, this balloon will float for a long distance. When it falls, it lets go of the seed as the wind moves it along the rough surface of the ground, and when it is thus unburdened the down fluffs out in every direction, making a perfect globe.

For the first season after the seed has rooted, the thistle develops only rosettes, meanwhile putting down roots and becoming permanently established. The next season, the flowers and seeds are developed, and then the plant dies. Would that this fact were true of the Canada thistle; but that, unfortunately, is perennial, and its persistent roots can only be starved out by keeping the stalks cut to the ground for the entire season. This thistle trusts to its extensively creeping rootstocks more than to its seeds for retaining its foothold and for

The Canada thistle

spreading. While it develops many seed balloons, a large number of its seeds are infertile and will not grow.

LESSON

Leading thought— The thistle is covered with sharp spines, and these serve to protect it from grazing animals. It has beautiful purple flowers, arranged in heads similar to those of the sunflower.

Method— A thistle plant brought into the schoolroom—root and all—and placed in water will serve well for this lesson. The questions should be given the pupils as to where thistles are found. Any thistle will do for the lesson.

Observations—

1. Where do you find the thistles growing? Do you find more than one species growing thickly together? Do you find any of the common thistles growing in soil which has been cultivated this season?

2. Describe the stalk, is it smooth? Is it weak or strong and woody? What sort of root has it?

3. Do the leaves grow alternately or opposite? Are they smooth or downy on one or both sides? Do the spines grow around the margins, or on the leaves and veins? Are the leaf edges flat, or wavy and ruffled?

4. How does this affect the direction in which the spines point? Are the leaves entire or deeply lobed? Have they petioles, or are they attached directly to the stalk?

5. Note if any buds or small branches nestle in the axils of the lower leaves. What effect does cutting the main stalk seem to have on each side shoot?

6. Do the flower-heads of the thistle grow singly or in clusters? Do they come from the summit of the stalk, or do they branch from its sides? Which blossom-heads open first—the topmost or those lowest on the stalk? Are the flowers fragrant? What insects do you most often see visiting thistle blossoms for pollen or nectar? Study the thistle flower according to the Lesson on page 99.

7. Carefully study a thistle balloon. How is the floss attached to the seed? Is it attached to the smaller, or the larger end? Hold the thistle balloon between your eye and the light. Does the down consist of single separate hairs, or have they many fine branches? How is the down arranged when all the flowers are packed together in the thistle-head? Take a seed from among its closely packed fellows in the thistle-head, and put it in the sun or in a warm, dry place where it cannot blow away. How long does it take for the balloon to open out? What is its shape? Is there any down at the center of the balloon or is it arranged in a funnel-shaped ring? Can you find a perfectly globular thistle balloon with the seeds still attached to it? How far do you think the thistle balloons might travel?

8. If a thistle seed finds a place for planting during the autumn, how does the young plant look the next season? Describe the thistle rosette. What growth does it make the second summer? What happens to it then?

9. Why can you not cultivate out the Canada thistles as you can the other species?

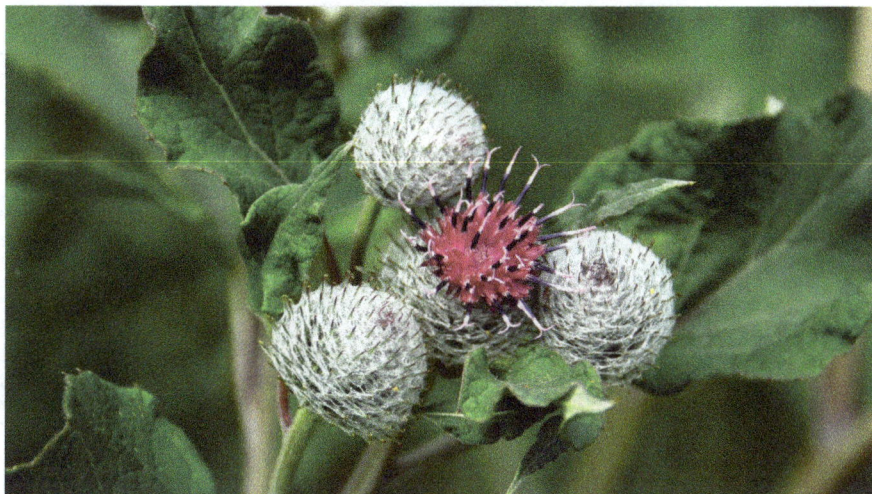

Burdock in bloom

The Burdock

TEACHER'S STORY

PSYCHOLOGISTS say that all young things are selfish, and the young burdock is a shining example of this principle. Its first leaves are broad and long, with long petioles by means of which they sprawl out from the growing stem in every direction, covering up and choking out all the lesser plants near them. In fact, the burdock remains selfish in this respect always, for its great basal leaves see to it that no other plants shall get the good from the soil near its own roots. One wonders at first how a plant with such large leaves can avoid shading itself; but there are some people very selfish toward the world who are very thoughtful of their own families, and the burdock belongs to this class. We must study carefully the arrangement of its leaves in order to understand its cleverness. The long basal leaves are stretched out flat; the next higher, somewhat smaller ones are lifted at a polite angle so as not to stand in their light. This courtesy characterizes all the leaves of the plant, for each higher leaf is smaller and has a shorter petiole, which is lifted at a narrower angle from the stalk; and all the leaves are so nicely adjusted as to form a pyramid, allowing the sunlight to sift down to each part. While some of the uppermost leaves may be

Burdock ready to seed

scarcely more than an inch long, the lower ones are very large. They are pointed at the tip and wide at the base; where the leaf joins the petiole it is irregular, bordered for a short distance on each side with a vein, and then finished with a "flounce," which is so full that it even reaches around the main stem—another device for getting more sunlight for itself and shutting it off from plants below. On the lower side, the leaf is whitish and feltlike to the touch; above it is a raw green, often somewhat smooth and shining. The leaf is in quality poor, coarse and flimsy, and it hangs—a web of shoddy—on its strong supporting ribs; lucky for it that its edges are slightly notched and much ruffled, else they would be torn and tattered. The petiole and stems are felty in texture; the petiole is grooved, and expands at its base to grasp the stems on both sides with a certain vicious pertinacity which characterizes the whole plant.

The flower-heads come off at the axils of the upper leaves, and are often so crowded that the leaf is almost lost to sight. It is amazing to behold the number of flower-heads which develop on one thrifty plant. The main stem and the pyramid of lower branching stems, are often crowded with the green balls beset with bracts which are hooked, spiny, and which hold safe the flowers. This composite flower-house is a fortress bristling with spears which are not changed to peaceful pruning-hooks, although they are hooked at the sharp end, every hook turning toward the flowers at the center; the lower bracts are shorter and stand out at right angles, while the others come off at lesser angles, graded so as to form a globular involucre—a veritable block-house. The flower might be a tidbit for the grazing animal; but, if so, he has never discovered it, for these protective hooks have kept him from ever enjoying a taste. The bracts protect, not only by hooks at the tip, but by spreading out at the bases so as to make a thickly battened dwelling for the flower-family.

A burdock floret with hooked bract.

But if we tear open one of these little fortresses, we are well repaid in seeing the quite pretty florets. The corollas are long, slender, pink tubes, with five, pointed lobes. The anther-tubes are purple, the pistils and the stigmas white; the stigmas are broad and feathery when they are dusting out the pollen from the anther-tubes, but later they change to very delicate pairs of curly Y's. The young seed is shining white, and the pappus forms a short, white fluff at the upper margin; but this is simply a family trait, for the burdock seeds never need to be ballooned to their destination; they have a surer method of travel. When in full bloom, the burdock flower-heads are very pretty and the skillful child weaver makes them into beautiful baskets. When I was a small girl, I made whole sets of furniture from these flowers; and then, becoming more ambitious, wove some into a coronet which I wore proudly for a few short hours, only to discover later, from my own experience, that great truth which Shakespeare voiced,—"uneasy lies the head that wears the crown."

In winter, the tough, gray stalks of the burdock still stand; although they may partially break, if they can thus better accomplish their purpose,—always falling toward the path. In this way, they may be sure of inserting the hooks of their seed storehouses into the clothing or covering of the passer-by; and when one gets a hold, mayhap a doz-

A butterfly helping to pollinate some burdock

en others will hold hands and follow. If they catch the tail of horse or cow, then indeed they must feel their destiny fulfilled; for the animal, switching about with its uneasy appendage, threshes out the seeds, and unheedingly plants them by trampling them into the ground. Probably some of the livestock of our Pilgrim Fathers came to America thus burdened; for the burdock is a European weed, although now it flourishes too successfully in America. The leaves of the burdock are bitter, and are avoided by grazing animals. Fortunately for us, certain flies and other insects like their bitter taste, and lay eggs upon them, which hatch into larvae that live all their lives between the upper and lower surfaces of the leaf. Often the leaves are entirely destroyed by the minute larvae of a fly, which live together cozily between these leaf blankets, giving the leaves the appearance of being afflicted with large blisters.

The burdocks have long vigorous taproots, and it is therefore difficult to eradicate them without much labor. But persistent cutting off the plant at the root will, if the cut be deep, finally discourage this determined weed.

LESSON

Leading thought— The burdock wins because its great leaves shade down plants in its vicinity, and also by having taproots. It scatters its seed by hooking its seed-heads fast to the passer-by.

Method— Study a healthy burdock plant in the field, to show how it shades down other plants and does not shade itself. The flowers and the seed-heads may be brought into the schoolroom for detailed study.

Observations—

1. Note a young plant. How much space do its leaves cover? Is anything growing beneath them? How are its leaves arranged to cover so much space? Of what advantage is this to the plant?

2. Study the full-grown plant. How are the lower leaves arranged? At what angles to the stalks do the petioles lie? Are the upper leaves as large as the lower ones? Do they stand at different angles to the stalk?

3. Study the arrangement of leaves on a burdock plant, to discover how it manages to shade down other plants with its leaves and yet does not let its own upper leaves shade those below.

4. Study a lower and an upper leaf. What is the general shape? What peculiarity where it joins the petiole? What is the texture of the leaf above and below? The color? Describe the petiole and how it joins the stem.

5. Where do the flowers appear on the stem? Are there many flowers developed? Count all the flower-heads on a thrifty burdock.

6. The burdock has its flowers gathered into families, like the sunflower and thistle. Describe the burdock flower-family according to the Lesson on page 99.

7. What insects visit the burdock flowers? Can you make baskets from the flower-heads?

8. Study the burdock again in winter, and see what has happened to it. Describe the seed and the seed-heads. How are the seed-heads carried far away from the parent plant? How many seeds in a single "house?" How do they escape?

9. Write the biography of a burdock plant which came to America as a seed, attached to the tail of a Shetland pony.

Prickly Lettuce, a Compass Plant

A close up of the underside of the prickly lettuce leaf

TEACHER'S STORY

THE more we know of plants, the more we admire their ways of attaining success in a world where it is only attained by a species after a long struggle. While plants may not be conscious of their own efforts for living on successfully, they have developed them just the same, and they merit our admiration perhaps even more, than as if their strategy was the result of conscious thought. The prickly lettuce has a story to tell us about success attained by the prevention of exhaustion from thirst. In fact, the success of this weed depends much upon its being able to live in dry situations and withstand the long droughts of late summer. The pale green stems grow up slim and tall, bearing leaves arranged alternately and from all sides, since between two, one of which is exactly above the other, two other leaves are borne. Thus, if the leaves stood out naturally, the shape of the whole plant would be a somewhat blunt pyramid. But during the hot, dry weather, the leaves do not stand out straight from the stem; instead, they twist about so that they are practically all in one plane, and usually point north and south, although this is not invariably the case. The way this twisting is accomplished is what interests us in this plant. The long spatulate

Notice the clasping stem of the leaf of prickly lettuce

leaf has a thick, fleshy midrib, and at the base are developed two pointed lobes which clasp the stalk. The leaf is soft and leathery and always seems succulent, because it retains its moisture; it has a ruffled edge near its base, which gives it room for turning without tearing its margin. Each leaf tips over sidewise toward the stem, and as far as necessary to bring one edge uppermost. Thus the sun cannot reach its upper surface to pump water from its tissues. The ruffled margin of the upper edge is pulled out straight when the leaf stands in this position, while the lower margin is more ruffled than ever. Thus, it stands triumphantly, turning edgewise to the sun, retaining its moisture and thriving when cultivated plants are dry and dying.

It also has another "anchor to the windward." A plant so full of juice would prove attractive food for cattle when pastures are dry. The leaves of this perhaps escape, because each has a row of very sharp spines on the lower side of the midrib. At first we might wonder why they are thus placed; but if we watch a grazing animal, as a cow, reach out her tongue to pull the herbage into her mouth, we see that these spines are placed where they will do the most efficient work. The teasel has the same clever way of warning off meddlesome tongues. The prickly lettuce also has spines on its stem, and the leaves are toothed with spines at their points.

LESSON

Leading thought— The sunshine sets the machinery in the leaf-factories going, and incidentally pumps up water from the soil, which pours out into the air from the leaves; but if the soil is dry the pump works just the same, and the plant thus robbed of its water soon withers and dies. The young plants of wild lettuce prevent the sun from pumping them dry during drought, by turning the edges of their leaves toward the sun, and thus not exposing the leaf surface to its rays. The leaves thus lifted stand in one plane. They are usually directed north and south. The lettuce also has spines to protect it from grazing animals.

Method— The lettuce should be studied in the field, and is a good subject for a lesson in late summer or September. This lesson should supplement the one on transpiration. The young plants show this arrangement of the leaves best. The flowers may be studied by the outline given in the Lesson on page 99.

Observations—

1. Where does the prickly lettuce grow? What sort of a stem has it? How are the leaves arranged on the stem?

2. If the leaves stood straight out from the stem, what would be the shape of the plant? How do the leaves stand? Is their upper surface exposed to the rays of the sun? Which portion of the leaf is turned toward the sun?

3. If the leaves turn sideways and stand in one plane, do they stand north and south or east and west? How does the edgewise position of the leaf protect the plant during drought? Why does any plant wither during drought? If the leaves of the lettuce should extend east and west instead of north and south, would they get more sun? (See lesson on the Sun.)

4. What is the shape of the lettuce leaf? How does it clasp the stalk? How is the base shaped so that the leaf can turn without tearing its edges? Sketch a leaf thus turned fully, showing how it is done. Does the leaf turn toward the stem or away from it?

5. How are the leaves protected against grazing cattle? How does the cow use her tongue to help bring herbage to her mouth? How are the prickly spines placed on the lettuce leaf, to make the cow's tongue uncomfortable? Sketch a leaf showing its shape, its venation and its spines.

The Dandelion

TEACHER'S STORY

THIS is the most persistent and indomitable of weeds, yet I think the world would be very lonesome without its golden flower-heads and fluffy seed-spheres. Professor Bailey once said that dandelions in his lawn were a great trouble to him until he learned to love them, and then the sight of them gave him keenest pleasure. And Lowell says of this "dear common flower"—

> " 'Tis Spring's largess, which she scatters now
> To rich and poor alike, with lavish hand;
> Though most hearts never understand
> To take it at God's value, and pass by
> The offered wealth with unrewarded eye."

It is very difficult for us, when we watch the behavior of the dandelions, not to attribute to them thinking power, they have so many ways of getting ahead of us. I always look at a dandelion and talk to it as if it were a real person. One spring when all the vegetables in my garden were callow weaklings, I found there, in their midst, a dandelion rosette with ten great leaves spreading out and completely shading a circle ten inches in diameter; I said, "Look here, Madam, this is my garden!" and I pulled up the squatter. But I could not help paying admiring tribute to the taproot, which lacked only an inch of being a foot in length. It was smooth, whitish, fleshy and, when cut, bled a milky juice showing that it was full of food; and it was as strong from the end-pull as a whipcord; it also had a bunch of rather fine rootlets about an inch below the surface of the soil and an occasional rootlet farther down; and then I said, "Madam, I beg your pardon; I think this was your garden and not mine."

Dandelion leaves afford an excellent study in variation of form. The edges of the leaf are notched in a peculiar way, so that the lobes were, by some one, supposed to look like lions' teeth in profile; thus the plant was called in France "dents-de-lion" (teeth of the lion), and we have made from this the name dandelion. The leaves are so bitter that grazing animals do not like to eat them, and thus the plants are safe even in pastures.

The hollow stem of the blossom-head from time immemorial has been a joy to children. It may be made into a trombone, which will give to the enterprising teacher an opportunity for a lesson in the physics of sound, since by varying its length, the pitch is varied. The dandelion-curls, which the little girls enjoy making, offer another lesson in physics—that of surface tension, too difficult for little girls to understand. But the action of this flower stem is what makes the dandelion seem so endowed with acumen. If the plant is in a lawn, the stem is short, indeed so short that the lawn-mower cannot cut off the flower-head. In this situation it will blossom and seed within two inches of the ground; but if the plant is in a meadow or in other high grass, the stem lifts up sometimes two feet or more, so that its blossom may be seen by bees and its seeds be carried off by the breeze without let or hindrance from the grass. We found two such stems each measuring over 30 inches in height.

Before a dandelion head opens, the stem, unless very short, is likely to bend down to protect the young flowers, but the night before it is to

Dandelion seeds being blown by the wind

bloom it straightens up; after the blossoms have matured it may again bend over, but straightens up when the seeds are to be cast off.

It often requires an hour for a dandelion head to open in the morning and it rarely stays open longer than five or six hours; it may require another hour to close. Usually not more than half the flowers of the head open the first day, and it may require several days for them all to blossom. After they have all bloomed and retired into their green house and put up the shutters, it may take them from one to two weeks to perfect their seeds.

In the life of the flower-head the involucre, or the house in which the flower family lives, plays an important part. The involucral bracts, in the row set next to the flowers, are sufficiently long to cover the unopened flowers; the bracts near the stem are shorter and curl back, making a frill. In the freshly opened flower-head, the buds at the middle all curve slightly toward the center, each bud showing a blunt, five-lobed tip which looks like the tips of five fingers held tightly together. The flowers in the outer row blossom first, straightening back and pushing the banner outward; and now we can see that the five lobes in the bud are the five notches at the end of the banner. All the flowers in the dandelion-head have banners, but those at the center, belonging to the younger flowers, have shorter and darker yellow banners. After a banner is unfurled, there pushes out from its tubular base a darker yellow anther-tube; the five filaments below the tube are visible with a lens. A little later, the stigma-ramrod pushes forth from the tube, its fuzzy sides acting like a brush to bring out all the pollen; later it rises far above the anther-tube and quirls back its stigma-lobes, as if every floret were making a dandelion curl of its own. The lens shows us, below the corolla, the seed. The pappus is not set in a collar upon the dandelion seed, as it is in the aster seed; there is a short stem above the seed which is called the "beak" and the pappus is attached to this.

Every day more blossoms open; but on dark, rainy days and during the night the little green house puts up its shutters around the flower-family, and if the bracts are not wide enough to cover the growing family, the banners of the outer flowers have thick or brownish portions along their lower sides which serve to calk the chinks. It is interesting to watch the dandelion stars close as the night falls, and still more interesting to watch the sleepy-heads awaken long after the sun is up in the morning; they often do not open until eight o'clock. The dandelion flower-families are very economical of their pollen and profuse nectar, and do not expose them until the bees and other insects are abroad ready to make morning calls.

After all the florets of a dandelion family have blossomed, they retire again into their green house and devote themselves to perfecting their seeds. They may stay thus in retirement for several days, and during this period the flower stem often grows industriously; and when the shutters of the little green house are again let down, what a different appearance has the dandelion family! The seeds with their balloons are set so as to make an exquisite, filmy globe; and now they are ready to coquette with the wind and, one after another, all the balloons go sailing off. One of these seeds is well worth careful observation through a lens. The balloon is attached to the top of the beak as an umbrella frame is attached to the handle, except that the "ribs" are many and fluffy; while the dandelion youngster, hanging below, has an overcoat armed with grappling hooks, which enable it to cling fast when the balloon chances to settle to the ground.

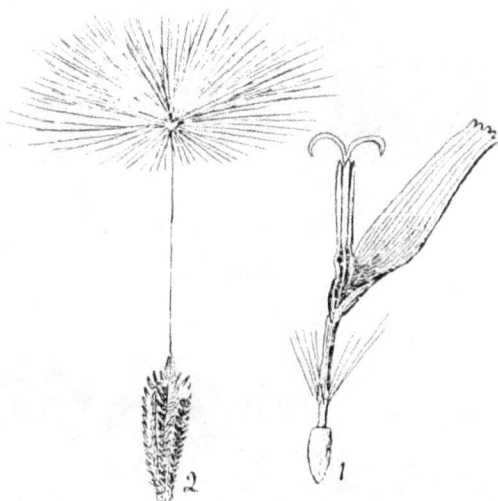

1. *Floret of dandelion; 2, seed of dandelion. Both enlarged.*

Father Tabb says of the dandelion,—"With locks of gold today; tomorrow silver gray; then blossom bald." But not the least beautiful part of the dandelion is this blossom-bald head after all the seeds are gone; it is like a mosaic, with a pit at the center of each figure where the seed was attached. There is an interesting mechanism connected with this receptacle.

Before the seeds are fully out this soon-to-be-bald head is concave at the center, later it becomes convex, and the mechanism of this movement liberates the seeds which are embedded in it.

Each freshly opened corolla-tube is full to overflowing with nectar, and much pollen is developed; therefore, the dandelion has many kinds of insect visitors. But perhaps the bee shows us best where the nectar is found; she thrusts her tongue down into the little tubes below the banners, working very rapidly from floret to floret. The dandelion stigmas have a special provision for securing cross-pollenation; and if that fails, to secure pollen from their own flower-family; and now the savants have found that the pistils can also grow seeds without any pollen from anywhere. It surely is a resourceful plant!

The following are the tactics by which the dandelion conquers us and takes possession of our lands: (a) It blossoms early in the spring and until snow falls, producing seed for a long season. (b) It is broadminded as to its location, and flourishes on all sorts of soils. (c) It thrusts its long tap-roots down into the soil, and thus gets moisture and food not reached by other plants. (d) Its leaves spread out from the base, and crowd and shade many neighboring plants out of existence. (e) It is on good terms with many insects, and so has plenty of pollen carriers to insure strong seeds; it can also develop seeds from its own pollen, and as a last resort it can develop seeds without any pollen.

(f) It develops almost numberless seeds, and the wind scatters them far and wide and they thus take possession of new territory. (g) It forms vigorous leaf-rosettes in the fall, and thus is able to begin growth early in the spring.

Dandelion in bloom

LESSON

Leading thought— The dandelions flourish despite our determined efforts to exterminate them. Let us study the way in which they conquer.

Method— The study should be made with the dandelions on the school grounds. Questions should be given, a few at a time, and then let the pupils consult the dandelions as to the answers. The dandelion is a composite flower and may be studied according to the Lesson on page 99. All the florets have banners or rays.

Observations—

1. Where do you find dandelions growing? If they are on the lawn, how long are their blossom or seed stems? If in a meadow or among high grass, how long is the blossom stem? Why is this? Is the blossom stem solid or hollow? Does it break easily?

2. Dig up a dandelion root and then explain why this weed withstands drought, and why it remains, when once planted.

3. Sketch or describe a dandelion leaf. Why was the plant named "lion's teeth?" How are the leaves arranged about the root? How does this help the dandelion and hinder other plants? In what condition do the leaves pass the winter under the snow? Why is this useful to the plant?

4. Take a blossom not yet open. Note the bracts that cover the unopened flower-head. Note the ones below and describe them.

5. Note the dandelion flower-head just open. Which flowers open

first? How do the buds look at the center? Do all the florets have banners? Are the banners of the central florets the same color and length as of those outside? Examine a floret and note the young seed. Is the pappus attached to it or above it?

6. What happens to the dandelion blossom on rainy or dark days? How is the dandelion family hidden during the rain? When does it appear again? Do you think that this has anything to do with the insect visitors? Do bees and other insects gather nectar during dark or rainy days?

7. Note at what hour the dandelions on the lawn go to sleep and at what hour they awaken on pleasant days.

8. Make notes on a certain dandelion plant three times a day: How long does it take the dandelion head to open fully on a sunny morning? How long does it remain open? How long does it take the flower-head to close? What proportion of the flowers in the head, blossoms during the first day? What proportion of the flowers in the head, blossoms during the second day? How long before they all blossom? Does the flower-head remain open longer in the afternoon on some days than on others, equally sunny? Does the stem bend over before the blossom-head opens?

9. After all the little flowers of a dandelion family have blossomed, what happens to it? How long does it stay shut up in its house? Measure the stem, and see if it stretches up during the time. How does the dandelion look when it opens again? Look at a dandelion-head full of seed, and see how the seeds are arranged to make a perfect globe. Shake the seeds off and examine the "bald head" with a lens. Can you see where the seeds were set?

10. Examine a dandelion seed with a lens. Describe the balloon, the beak or stem of the balloon, and the seed. Why do you suppose the seed has these hooks?

11. How early in the spring, and how late in the fall, do dandelions blossom?

12. Watch a bee when she is working on a dandelion flower, and see where she thrusts her tongue and which flowers she probes.

13. Tell all the things that you can remember which the dandelion does in order to live and thrive in spite of us.

14. What use do we make of the dandelions?

The Pearly Everlasting

THESE wraithlike flowers seem never to have been alive, rather than to have been endowed with everlasting life. The cattle share this opinion and would no sooner eat these plants than if they were made of cotton batting. The stems are covered with white felt; the long narrow leaves are very pale green, and when examined with a lens, look as if they were covered with a layer of cotton which disguises all venation except the thick midrib. The leaves are set alternate, and become shorter and narrower and whiter toward the top of the plant, where they are obliged to give their sustenance to the flower stems borne in their axils. All this cottony covering has its uses to prevent the evaporation of water from the plant during the long droughts. The everlasting never has much juice in its leaves but what it has, it keeps.

The flower stems are rather stout, woolly, soft and pliable. They come off at the axils of the threadlike whitish leaves. The pistillate and

158

1. Pistillate floret, 2. pappus, 3. staminate floret. All enlarged.

the staminate flowers are borne on separate plants, and usually in separate patches. The pistillate, or seed-developing, plants have globular flower buds, almost egg-shaped, with a fluffy lemon-yellow knob at the tip; this fluff is made up of stigmas split at the end. At the center of this tassel of lemon-yellow stigma-plush, may often be seen a depression; at the bottom of this well, there are three or four perfect flowers. One of the secrets of the everlasting is, evidently, that it does not put all of its eggs in one basket; it has a few perfect flowers for insurance. This pistillate or seed-bearing flower has a long, delicate tube, ending in five needlelike points and surrounded by a pretty pappus. The bracts of the flower-cluster seem to cling around the base of the beautiful yellow tassel of fertile flowers, as if to emphasize it. They look as if they were made of white Japanese paper, and when looked at through a lens, they resemble the petals of a water lily. They are dry to begin with, so they cannot wither.

The staminate, or pollen-bearing, flower-heads are like white birds' nests, the white bracts forming the nest and the little yellow flowers the eggs. The flower has a tubular, five-pointed starlike corolla, with five stamens joined in a tube at the middle, standing up like a barrel from the corolla. The anther-tube is ocher-yellow with brown stripes, and is closed at first with five little flaps, making a cone at the top. Later, the orange-yellow pollen bulges out as if it were boiling over. The flowers around the edges of the flower-disk open first.

LESSON

Leading thought— There are often found growing on the poor soil in dry pastures, clumps of soft, whitish plants which are never eaten by cattle. There is so little juice in them that they retain their form when dried and thus have won their name.

Method— The pupils should see these plants growing, so that they may observe the staminate and pistillate flowers, which are on separate plants and in separate clumps. If this is not practicable, bring both kinds of flowers into the schoolroom for study.

Observations—

1. Where does the pearly everlasting grow? Do cattle eat it?

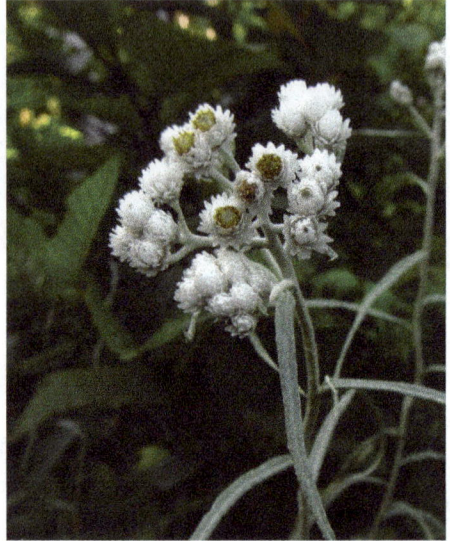

Why is this? What is the general color of the plant? What is the stem covered with?

2. What is the shape of the leaves? How are they veined? With what are they covered? How are they placed on the stem? What is the relative size of the lower and upper leaves? Why is there a difference?

3. Do you see some plants which have egg-shaped blossoms, each with a yellow knob at the tip? Take one apart and look at it with a lens, and see what forms the white part and what forms the yellow knob. Do you see other flowers that look like little white birds' nests filled with yellow eggs? Look at one of them with a lens, and tell what kind of a flower it is.

4. Except that the pistillate and staminate flowers are on different plants, the flowers of the pearly everlasting should be studied according to the Lesson on page 99.

5. What do you know of the edelweiss of the Alps? How does it resemble the pearly everlasting? Do you know another common kind of everlasting called pussy's toes?

Mullein

TEACHER'S STORY

"I like the plants that you call weeds,—
Sedge, hardhack, mullein, yarrow,—
Which knit their leaves and sift their seeds
Where any grassy wheel-track leads
Through country by-ways narrow."

—LUCY LARCOM.

WE take much pride unto ourselves because we belong to the chosen few of the "fittest," which have survived in the struggle for existence. But, if we look around upon other members of this select band, we shall find many lowly beings which we do not ordinarily recognize as our peers. Mullein is one of them, and after we study its many ways of "winning out" then may we bow to it and call it "brother."

I was wandering one day in a sheep pasture and looking curiously at the few plants left uneaten. There was a great thistle with its sharp spines and the pearly everlasting—too woolly and anaemic to be ap-

161

See the felt-like leaves of the mullein

petizing even to a sheep; and besides these, there was an army of mullein stalks—tall, slim, and stiff-necked, or branching like great candelabra, their upper leaves adhering alternately to the stalks for half their length. I stopped before one of them and mentally asked, "Why do the sheep not relish you? Are you bitter?" I took a bite, Nebuchadnezzar-like, and to my untrained taste it seemed as good fodder as any; but my tongue smarted and burned for some time after, from being pricked by the felt which covered the leaf. I recalled the practical joke of which my grandmother once made me the victim; she told me that to be beautiful, I needed only to rub my cheeks with mullein leaves, an experience which convinced me that there were other things far more desirable than beauty—comfort, for instance. This felt on the mullein is beautiful, when looked at through a microscope; it consists of a fretwork of little, white, sharp spikes. No wonder my cheeks were red one day and purple the next, and no wonder the sheep will not eat it unless starved! This frostlike felt covering not only keeps the mullein safe from grazing animals but it also keeps the water from evaporating from the leaf and this enables the plant to withstand drought. I soon discovered another means devised by the mullein for this same purpose, when I tried to dig up the plant with a stick; I followed its tap-root down far enough to understand that it was a sub-soiler and reached below most other plants for moisture and food. Although it was late autumn, the mullein was still in blossom; there were flowers near the tip and also one here and there on the seed-crowded stem. I estimated there were hundreds of seed-capsules on that one plant; I opened one, still covered with the calyx-lobes, and found that the mullein was still battling for survival; for I found this capsule and many others inhabited by little brown-headed white grubs, which gave an exhibition of

St. Vitus dance as I laid open their home. They were the young of a snout beetle, which is a far more dangerous enemy of the mullein than is the sheep.

The mullein plant is like the old woman who lived in a shoe in the matter of blossom-children; she has so many that they are unkempt and irregular, but there are normally four yellow or white petals and a five-lobed calyx. I have never been able to solve the problem of the five stamens which, when the flower opens, are folded together in a knock-kneed fashion. The upper three are bearded below the anthers, the middle being the shortest. The lower two are much longer and have no fuzz on their filaments; they at first stand straight out, with the stigma between them; but after the upper anthers have shed their pollen, these stamens curve up like boars' teeth and splash their pollen on the upper petals, the stigma protruding desolately and one-sidedly below. Later the corolla, stamens and all, falls off, leaving the stigma and style attached to the seed-capsule.

The color of the mullein flowers varies from lemon-yellow to white. The filaments are pale yellow; the anthers and pollen, orange. The seed-capsule is encased in the long calyx-lobes, and is shaped like a blunt egg. Cutting it in two crosswise, the central core, tough and flattened and almost filling the capsule, is revealed and, growing upon its surface, are numberless tiny, brown seeds, as fine as gunpowder. Later the capsule divides partially in quarters, opening wide enough to shake out the tiny seeds with every wandering blast. The seed, when seen through a lens, is very pretty; it looks like a section of a corncob, pitted and ribbed. A nice point of investigation for some junior naturalist is to work out the fertilization of the mullein flower, and note

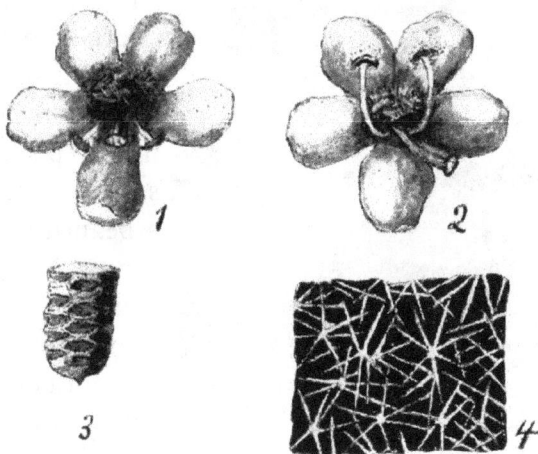

1, 2. Mullein flowers in different stages. 3. Mullein seed enlarged. 4. A bit of Mullein leaf enlarged.

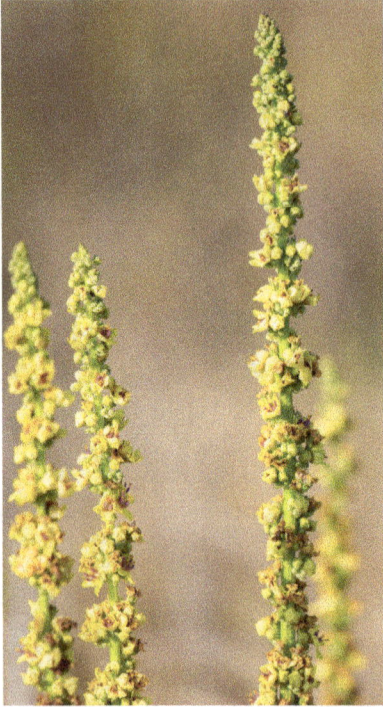

what insects assist. The mullein has another spoke in the wheel of its success. The seed, scattered from the sere and dried plants, settles comfortably in any place where it can reach the soil, and during the first season grows a beautiful velvety rosette of frosted leaves. No wonder Europeans grow it in gardens under the name of the "American velvet plant." These rosettes lie flat under the snow, with their taproots strong and already deep in the soil, and are ready to begin their work of food-making as soon as the spring sun gives them power.

LESSON

Leading thought— The mullein has its leaves covered with felt, which prevents evaporation during the dry weather and also prevents animals from grazing upon the plant. It has a deep root, and this gives moisture and food beyond the reach of most other plants. It blossoms all summer and until the snow comes in the autumn, and thus forms many, many seeds, which the wind plants for it; and here in our midst it lives and thrives despite us.

Method— The pupils should have a field trip to see what plants are left uneaten in pastures, and thus learn where mullein grows best. The flower or seed stalk, with basal leaves and root, may be brought to the schoolroom for the lesson.

Observations—

1. Where does the mullein grow? Do you ever see it in swamps or woodlands? Do cattle or sheep eat it? Why? Does it flourish during the summer drought? How is it clothed to prevent the evaporation of its sap? Look at a mullein leaf with a lens and describe its appearance.

2. What sort of a root has the mullein? How is its root adapted to get moisture and plant food which other plants cannot reach? De-

scribe the flowering stalk. How are the leaves arranged on it and attached to it? Are there several branching flower stalks or a single one?

3. Describe the flower bud. Do the mullein flowers nearest the base or the tip begin to blossom first? Is this invariable, or do flowers open here and there irregularly on the stem during the season?

4. Describe the mullein flower. How many lobes has the calyx? Are these covered with felt? How many petals? Are there always this number? Are the petals of the same size? Are they always regular in shape?

5. How many stamens? How do the upper three differ from the lower two? Describe the style and stigma. What are the colors of petals, anthers and stigma? What insects do you find visiting the flowers?

6. Describe the seed-capsule, its shape and covering. Cut it across and describe the inside. Where are the seeds borne? Are there many? Look at the seed with a lens, and describe it. How does the capsule open and by what means are the seeds scattered?

7. Does the mullein grow from the seed to maturity in one year? How does it look at the end of the first season? Describe the winter rosette, telling how it is fitted to live beneath the snows of winter. What is the advantage of this habit?

8. Write a theme telling all the ways the mullein has of flourishing and of combating other plants.

> "The mullein's pillar, tipped with golden flowers,
> Slim rises upward, and yon yellow bird
> Shoots to its top."
> —"THE HILL HOLLOW," A. B. STREET.

> "Sober dress never yet made you sullen,
> Style or size never brought you a blush;
> You're the envy of weavers, O, Mullein,
> For no shuttle can mimic your plush.
> With your feet in the sand you were born,
> Woolly monk of the thorn-field and fallow,
> But your heart holds the milk of the mallow,
> And your head wears the bloom of the corn."
> —THERON BROWN.

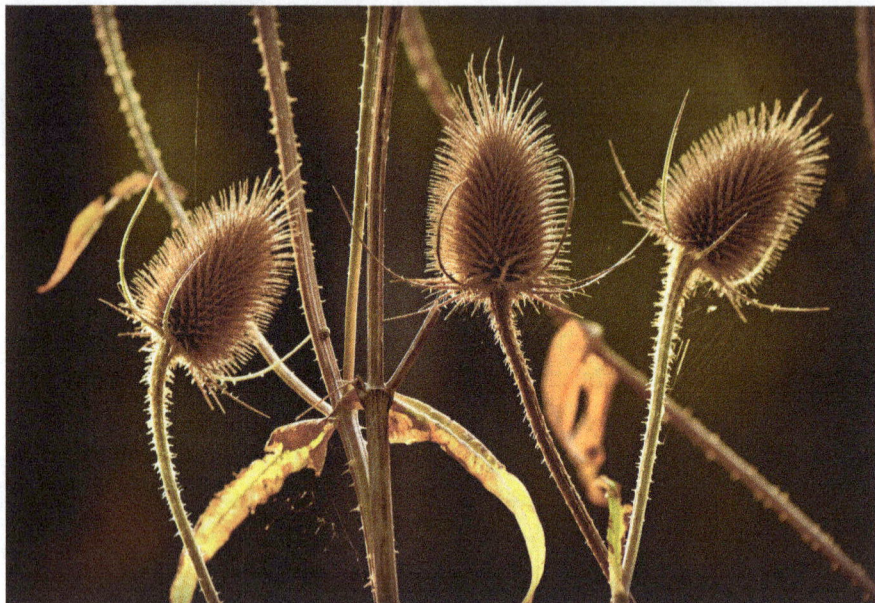

The Teasel

TEACHER'S STORY

THE old teasel stalks standing gaunt and gray in the fields, braving the blasts of winter, seem like old suits of armor, which elicit admiration from us for the strength and beauty of the protecting visor, breast-plate and gauntlets, and at the same time veer our thoughts to the knights of old who once wore them in the fray. Thus, with the teasel, we admire this panoply of spears, and they recall the purple flowers and the ribbed seeds which were once the treasure of every spear-guarded cavity and the proud reason of every lance at rest.

Let us study this plant in armor: First, its stem is tough, woody, hollow, with ridges extending its full length and each ridge armed with spines which are quite wide at the base and very sharp. It is impossible to take hold anywhere without being pricked by either large or small spines. The leaves are just fitted for such a stem. They are long, lanceolate, set opposite in pairs, rather coarse in texture, with a stiff, whitish midrib; the bases of the two leaves closely clasp the stem; the midrib is armed below with a row of long, white, recurved prickers, and woe unto the tongue of grazing beast that tries to lift this leaf into the mouth. If one pair of clasping leaves point east and west, the next pairs above and below point north and south.

The flower stems come off at the axils of the leaves and therefore each pair stands at right angles to the ones above and below. But if the teasel protects its stem and leaves with spikes, it does more for its flowers, which are set in dense heads armed with spines, and the head is set in an involucre of long, upcurving spiny prongs. If we look at it carefully, the teasel flower-head wins our admiration, because of the exquisite geometrical design made by the folded bases of the spines, set in diagonal rows. If we pull out a spine, we find that it enlarges toward the base to a triangular piece that is folded at right angles for holding the flower. Note that the spiny bracts at the tip of the flower-head are longer and more awesome than those at the sides; if we pass our hands down over the flower-head we feel how stiff the spines, or bracts are, and can hear them crackle as they spring back.

The teasel has a quite original method of blossoming. The golden-rod begins to blossom at the tip of the flowering branches and the blossom-tide runs inward and downward toward the base. The clover begins at the base and blossoms toward the tip, or the center. But the teasel begins at the middle and blossoms both ways, and how it knows just where to begin is more than we can tell. But some summer morning we will find its flower-head girt about its middle with a wide band of purple blossoms; after a few days, these fade and drop off, and then there are two bands, sometimes four rows of flowers in each, and sometimes only two. Below the lower band and above the upper band, the enfolding bracts are filled with little, round-headed lilac buds, while between the two rows of blossoms the protecting bracts hold the precious growing seed. Away from each other this double procession moves, until the lower band reaches the pronged involucre and the upper one forms a solid patch on the apex of the flower-head. Since the secondary blossom-heads starting from the leaf axils are younger, we may find all stages of this blossoming in the flower-heads of one plant.

No small flower pays better for close examination than does that of the teasel. If we do not pull the flower-head apart, what we see is a lit-

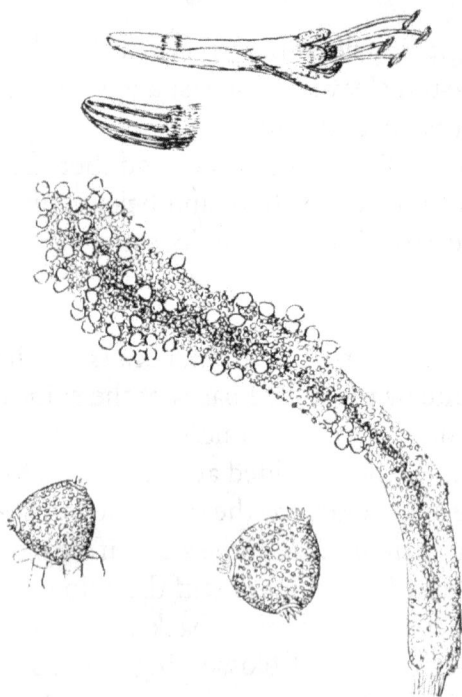

Teasel flower and seed enlarged. The stigma of a teasel floret much magnified to show the pollen adhering to it. Below, are pollen grains greatly magnified.

tle purple flower consisting of a white tube with four purple lobes at the end, the lower lobe being a little longer than the others and turning up slightly at its tip; projecting from between each of the lobes, and fastened to the tube, are four stamens with long, white filaments and beautiful purple anthers filled with large, pearly white pollen grains; at the very heart of the flower, the white stigma may be seen far down the tube. But a little later, after the anthers have fallen or shriveled, the white stigma extends out of the blossom like a long, white tongue and is crowded with white pollen grains.

But to see the flower completely we need to break or cut a flower-head in two. Then we see that the long white tube is tipped at one end with purple lobes and a fringe of anthers, and at the other is set upon a little green, fluffy cushion which caps the ovary; the shape of the ovary in the flower tells us by its form how the seed will look later. Enfolding ovary and tube is the bract with its spiny edges, pushing its protecting spear outward, but not so far out as the opening of the flower, for that might keep away the insects which carry the teasel's pollen. The pollen of the teasel is white and globular, with three little rosettes arranged at equal distances upon it like a bomb with three fuses. These little rosettes are the growing points of the pollen grains and from any of them may emerge the pollen tube to push down into the stigma. The teasel pollen is an excellent subject for the children to study, since it is so very large; and if examined with a microscope with a three-fourths objective, the tubes running from the pollen grains into the stigma may be easily seen.

Teasel in bloom

In blossoming, the teasel does not always seem to count straight in the matter of rows of flowers. There may be more rows in the upper band than in the lower, or *vice versa;* this is especially true of the smaller secondary blossoms. But though the teasel flowers fade and the leaves fall off, still the spiny skeleton stands, the thorny stalks holding up the empty flower-heads like candelabra, from which the seeds are tossed far and wide, shaken out by the winds of autumn. But though battered by wintry blasts, the teasel staunchly stands; even until the ensuing summer, each bract on guard and its heart empty where once was cherished blossom and seed. Alas, because of this emptiness, it has been debased by practical New England housewives into a utensil for sprinkling clothes for ironing.

The spines of one species of teasel were, in earlier times, used for raising the nap on woolen cloth, and the plant was grown extensively for that purpose. The bees are fond of the teasel blossoms and teasel honey has an especially fine flavor.

The teasels are biennial, and during the first season, develop a rosette of crinkled leaves which have upon them short spines.

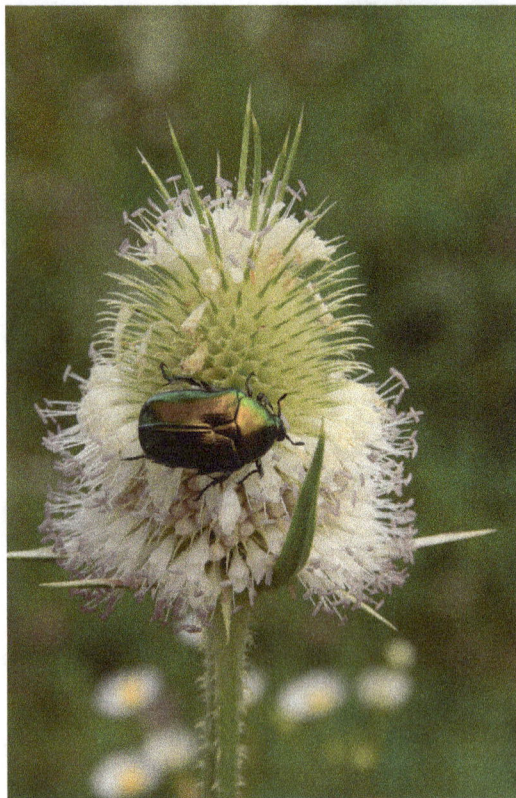

Leading thought— The teasel is a plant in armor, so protected that it can flourish and raise its seeds in pastures where cattle graze. It has a peculiar method of beginning to blossom in the middle of the flower-head and then blossoming upward and downward from this point.

Method— In September, bring in a teasel plant which shows all stages of blossoming, and let the pupils make observations in the schoolroom.

Observations—

1. Where does the teasel grow? Is it ever eaten by cattle? Why not? How is it protected?

2. What sort of stem has it? Is it hollow or solid? Where upon it are the spines situated? Are the spines all of the same size? Can you take hold of the stem anywhere without being pricked?

3. What is the shape of the leaves? How do they join the stem? Are the leaves set opposite or alternate? If one pair points east and west in which direction will the pairs above and below point? How and where are the leaves armed? How does the cow or sheep draw the leaves into the mouth with the tongue? If either should try to do this with the teasel, how would the tongue be injured?

4. Where do the flower stems come off? Do they come off in pairs? How are the pairs set in relation to each other?

5. What is the general appearance of the teasel flower-head? Describe the long involucre prongs at the base. If the teasel is in blossom, where do you find the flowers? How many girdles of flowers are there

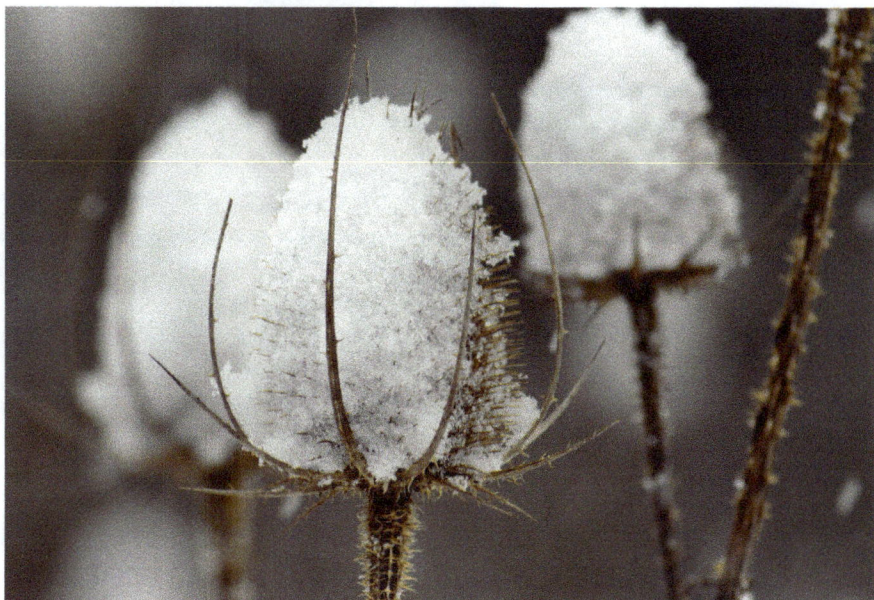

around the flower-head? How many rows in one girdle? Where did the first flowers blossom in the teasel flower-head? Where on the head will the last blossoms appear? Where are the buds just ready to open? Where are the ripened seeds?

6. Examine a single flower. How is it protected? Cut out a flower and bract and see how the long-spined bract enfolds it. Is the bract spear long enough to keep the cattle from grazing on the blossom? Is it long enough to keep the bees and other insects from visiting the flowers? Where are the longest spines on the teasel head?

7. Study a single flower. What is the shape of its corolla? How is it colored? What color are the stamens? How many? Describe the pollen. If the pollen is being shed where is the stigma? After the pollen is shed, what happens to the stigma?

8. What do you find at the base of the flower? How does the young seed look? Later in the season take a teasel head and describe how it scatters its seed. How do the ripe seeds look? How long will the old teasel plants stand?

9. For what were teasels once used? How many years does a teasel plant live? How does it look at the end of its first season? How is this an advantage as a method of passing the winter?

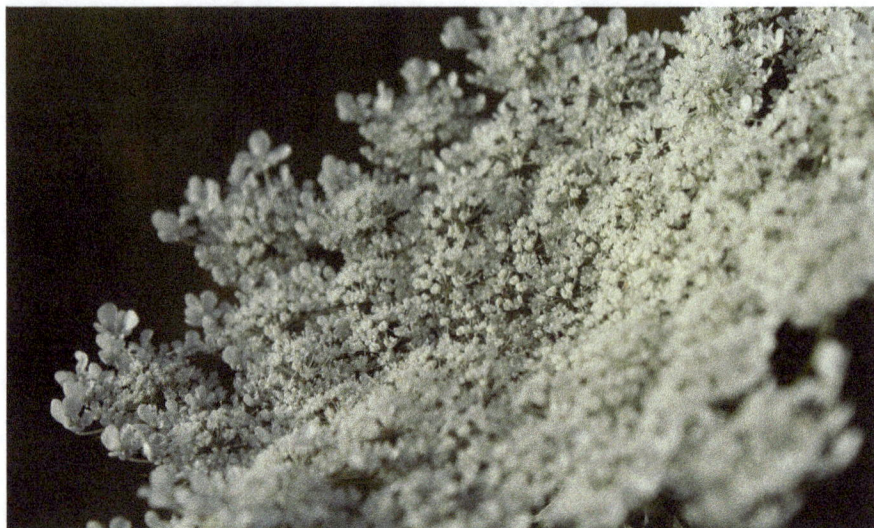

Queen Anne's Lace, or Wild Carrot

QUEEN ANNE was apparently given to wearing lace made in medallion patterns; and even though we grant that her lace is most exquisite in design as well as in execution, we wish most sincerely that there had been established in America such a high tariff on this royal fabric as to have prohibited its importation. It has for decades held us and our lands prisoners in its delicate meshes, it being one of the most stubborn and persistent weeds that ever came to us from over the seas.

But for those people who admire lace of intricate pattern, and beautiful blossoms whether they grow on scalawag plants or not, this medallion flower attributed to Queen Anne is well worth studying. It belongs to the family *Umbelliferae*, which one of my small pupils always called umbrelliferae because, he averred, they have umbrella blossoms. In the case of Queen Anne's lace the flower-cluster, or umbel, is made up of many smaller umbels, each a most perfect flower-cluster in itself. Each tiny white floret has five petals and should have five stamens with creamy anthers, but often has only two. However, it has always at its center two fat little pistils set snugly together, and it rests in a solid, bristly, green, cup-like calyx. Twenty or thirty of these little blossoms are set in a rosette, the stems of graded length; and where the bases of the stems meet are some long, pointed, narrow bracts, which protectingly brood the flowers in the bud and the seeds as they ripen. Each of these little flower-clusters, or umbels, has a long stem, its length being just fit to bring it to its right place in the medallion pattern of this royal lace. And these stems also have set at their bases some bracts with long, thread-like lobes, which make a delicate, green background for the opening blossoms; these bracts curl up protectingly about the buds and the seeds. If we look straight into the large flower-cluster, we can see that each component cluster, or umbelicel, seems to have its own share in making the larger pattern; the outside blossoms of the outside clusters have the outside petals larger, thus forming a beautiful border and calling to mind the beautiful flowers of the Composites. At the very center of this flower medallion, there is often a larger floret with delicate wine-colored petals; this striking floret is not a part of a smaller flower-cluster, but stands in stately solitude upon its own isolated stem. The reason for this giant floret at the center of the wide, circular flower-cluster is a mystery; and so far as I know, the botanists have not yet explained the reason for its presence. May we not, then, be at liberty to explain its origin on the supposition that her Royal Highness, Queen Anne, was wont to fasten her lace medallions upon her royal person with garnet-headed pins?

When the flowers wither and the seeds begin to form, the flower-cluster then becomes very secretive; every one of the little umbels turns toward the center, its stem curving over so that the outside umbels reach over and "tuck in" the whole family; and the threadlike bracts at the base reach up as if they, too, were in the family councils, and must do their slender duty in helping to make the fading flowers into a little, tightfisted clump; and all of this is done so that the precious seeds may be safe while they are ripening. Such little porcupines as these seeds are! Each seed is clothed with long spines set in bristling rows, and is a most forbidding-looking youngster when examined through a lens; and yet there is method in its spininess, and we must grudgingly grant that it is not only beautiful in its ornamentation but is also well fitted to take hold with a will when wandering winds sift it down to the soil.

The wild carrot is known in some localities as the "bird's-nest weed," because the maturing seed-clusters, their edges curving inward, look like little birds' nests. But no bird's nest ever contained so many eggs as does this imitation one. In one we counted 34 tiny umbels on which ripened 782 seeds; and the plant, from which this "bird's nest" was taken, developed nine more quite as large.

Altogether the wild carrot is well fitted to maintain itself in the struggle for existence, and is most successful in crowding out its betters in pasture and meadow. Birds do not like its spiny seeds; the stem of the plant is tough and its leaves are rough and have an unpleasant odor and acrid taste, which render it unpalatable to grazing animals. Winter's cold cannot harm it, for it is a biennial; its seeds often germinate in the fall, sending down long, slender taproots crowned with tufts of inconspicuous leaves; it thus stores up a supply of starchy food which enables it to start early the next season with great vigor. The root, when the plant is fully grown, is six or eight inches long, as thick as a finger and yellowish white in color; it is very acrid and somewhat poisonous.

The surest way of exterminating the Queen Anne's lace is to prevent its prolific seed production by cutting or uprooting the plants as soon as the first blossoms open.

> " 'Tis Eden everywhere to hearts that listen
> And watch the woods and meadows grow."
>
> —Theron Brown.

Lesson

Leading thought— Queen Anne's lace is a weed which came to us from Europe and flourishes better here than on its native soil. It has beautiful blossoms set in clusters, and it matures many seeds which it manages to plant successfully.

Method— The object of this lesson should be to show the pupils how this weed survives the winter and how it is able to grow where it is not wanted, maintaining itself successfully, despite man's enmity. The weed is very common along most country roadsides, and in many pastures and meadows. It blossoms very late in the autumn, and is

Queen Anne's lace in its natural habitat

available for lessons often as late as November. Its seed-clusters may be used for a lesson at almost any time during the winter.

Observations—

1. Look at a wild carrot plant; how are its blossoms arranged? Take a flower-cluster, what is its shape? How many small flower-clusters make the large one? How are these arranged to make the large cluster symmetrical?

2. Take one of the little flower-clusters from near the center, and one from the outside, of the large cluster; how many little flowers, or florets make up the smaller cluster? Look at one of the florets through a lens; can you see the cup-shaped calyx? How many petals has it? Can you see its five anthers and its two white pistils?

3. Take one of the outer florets of the outside cluster; are all its flowers the same shape? How do they differ? Where are the florets with the large petals placed in the big flower-cluster? How does this help to make "the pattern?"

4. Do the outside or the central flowers of the large clusters open first? Can you find a cluster with an almost black or very dark red floret at its center? Is this dark flower a part of one of the little clusters

175

or does it stand alone, its stem reaching directly to the main stalk? Do you think it makes the flowers of the Queen Anne's lace prettier to have this dark red floret at the center?

5. Take a flower-cluster with the flowers not yet open. Can you see the threadlike green bracts that close up around each bud? Can you see finely divided, threadlike bracts that stand out around the whole cluster? What position do these bracts assume when the flowers are open? What do they do after the flowers fade and the seeds are being matured?

6. What is the general shape of the seed-cluster of the wild carrot? Have you ever found such a cluster broken off and blowing across the snow? Do you think this is one way the seed is planted?

7. Examine a single seed of the wild carrot with a lens. Is it round or oblong? Thin or flat? Is it ridged or grooved? Has it any hooks or spines by which it might cling to the clothing of passers-by, or to the hair or fleece of animals, and thus be scattered more widely? Does the seed cling to its stem or break away readily when it is touched?

8. Take one seed-cluster and count the number of seeds within it. How many seed-clusters do you find on a single plant? How many seeds do you, therefore, think a single plant produces?

9. What should you consider the best means of destroying this prolific weed?

10. What do you think is the reason that the wild carrot remains untouched, so that it grows vigorously and matures its seeds in lanes and pastures where cattle graze?

11. Have you noticed any birds feeding on the seeds of the wild carrot?

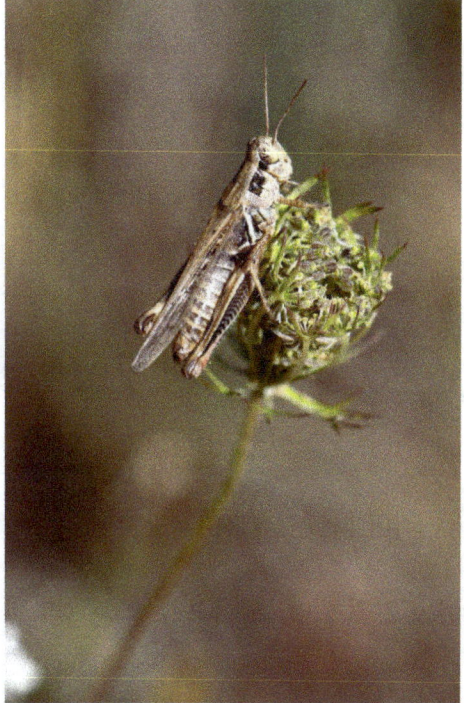

I do not want change: I want the same old and loved things, the same wild flowers, the same trees and soft ash-green; the turtle-doves, the blackbirds, the coloured yellowhammer sing, sing, singing so long as there is light to cast a shadow on the dial, for such is the measure of his song, and I want them in the same place. Let me find them morning after morning, the starry-white petals radiating, striving upwards to their ideal. Let me see the idle shadows resting on the white dust; let me hear the humble-bees, and stay to look down on the rich dandelion disc. Let me see the very thistles opening their great crowns—I should miss the thistles; the reed-grasses hiding the moor-hen; the bryony bine, at first crudely ambitious and lifted by force of youthful sap straight above the hedgerow to sink of its own weight presently and progress with crafty tendrils; swifts shot through the air with outstretched wings like crescent-headed shaftless arrows darted from the clouds; the chaffinch with a feather in her bill; all the living staircase of the spring, step by step, upwards to the great gallery of the summer—let me watch the same succession year by year.

—"The Pageant of Summer," by Richard Jeffries.

CULTIVATED
CROPS

The Clovers

TEACHER'S STORY
"Sweet by the roadside, sweet by the rills,
Sweet in the meadows, sweet on the hills,
Sweet in its wine, sweet in its red,
Oh, half of its sweetness cannot be said;
Sweet in its every living breath,
Sweetest, perhaps, at last, in death."
—"A SONG OF CLOVER," HELEN HUNT JACKSON.

CLOVER has for centuries been a most valuable forage crop; and for eons it has been the special partner of the bees, giving them honey for their service in carrying its pollen; and in recent years it has been discovered that it has also formed a mysterious and undoubtedly an ancient partnership with bacteria below ground, which, moreover, brings fertility to the soil. The making of a collection of the clovers of a region is a sure way of enlisting the pupils' interest in these valuable plants. The species have some similarities and differences, which give

181

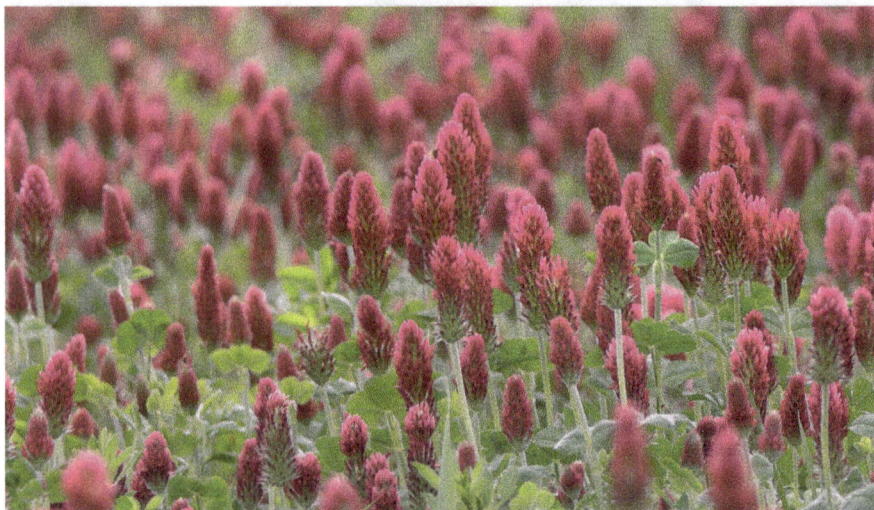
A field of clover

opportunity for much observation in comparing them. There may be found in most localities the white and yellow sweet clovers, the black and spotted medics and their relative the alfalfa; while of the true clovers there are the red, the zigzag, the buffalo, the rabbit's foot, the white, the alsike, the crimson, and two yellow or hop clovers.

In all the clovers, those blossoms which are lowest, or on the outside of the head, blossom first, and all of them have upon their roots the little swellings, or nodules, which are the houses in which the beneficent bacteria grow.

If we pull up or dig out the roots of alfalfa, or of the true clovers or vetches, we find upon the rootlets little swellings which are called nodules, or root-tubercles. Although these tubercles look so uninteresting, no fairy story was ever more wonderful than is theirs. They are, in fact, the home of the clover brownies, which help the plants to do their work. Each nodule is a nestful of living beings, so small that it would take twenty-five thousand of them end to end to reach an inch; therefore, even a little swelling can hold many of these minute organisms, which are called bacteria. For many years people thought that these swellings were injurious to the roots of the clover, but now we know that the bacteria which live in them are simply underground partners of these plants. The clover roots give the bacteria homes and place to grow, and in return these are able to extract a very valuable chemical fertilizer from the air, and to change its form so that the clovers can absorb it. The name of this substance is nitrogen, and it makes up more than three-fourths of the air we breathe. Other plants are unable to take the nitrogen from the air and use it for food, but these little bacteria extract it from the air which fills every little space between every two grains of soil and then change it to

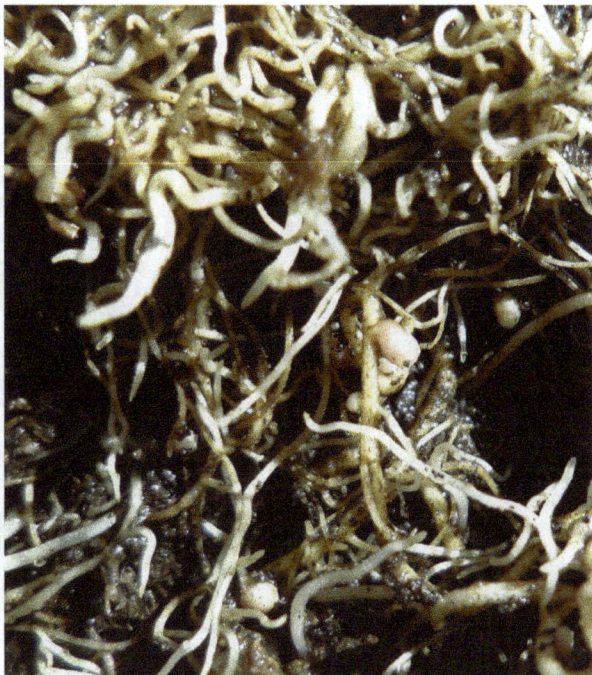

White clover roots showing nodules or root tubercles

a form which the clovers can use. After the clover crop is harvested, the roots remain in the ground, their little storehouses filled with this precious substance, and the soil falls heir to it.

Nitrogen in the form of commercial fertilizer is the most expensive which the farmer has to buy. So when he plants clover or alfalfa on his land, he is bringing to the soil this expensive element of plant growth, and it costs him nothing. This is why a good farmer practices the rotation of crops and puts clover upon his land every three or four years.

Alfalfa is so dependent on its little underground partners, that it cannot grow without them; and so the farmer plants, with the alfalfa seed, some of the soil from an old alfalfa field, which is rich in these bacteria. On a farm I know, the bacterial soil gave out before all of the seed was planted; and when the crop was ready to cut it was easy to see just where the seed without the inoculated soil had been planted, for the plants that grew there were small and poor, while the remainder of the field showed a luxurious growth.

Alfalfa blossoms

It is because of the great quantity of nitrogen absorbed from the air through the bacteria on its roots that the alfalfa is such a valuable fodder; for it contains the nitrogen which otherwise would have to be furnished to cattle in expensive grain or cotton-seed meal. The farmer who gives his stock alfalfa does not need to pay such large bills for grain. Other plants belonging to the same family as the clovers—like the vetches and cow-peas—also have bacteria on their roots. But each species of legume has its own species of bacteria; although in some cases soil inoculated with bacteria from one species of legume will grow it on roots of another species. Thus, the bacteria on the roots of sweet clover will grow on the roots of alfalfa and many farmers use the soil inoculated by sweet clover to start their alfalfa crops.

In addition to the enriching of the soil, clover roots, which penetrate very deeply, protect land from being washed away by freshets and heavy rains; and since clover foliage makes a thick carpet over the surface of the soil, it prevents evaporation and thus keeps the soil moist. Crimson clover is used extensively as a cover crop; it is sowed in the fall, especially where clean culture is practiced in orchards,

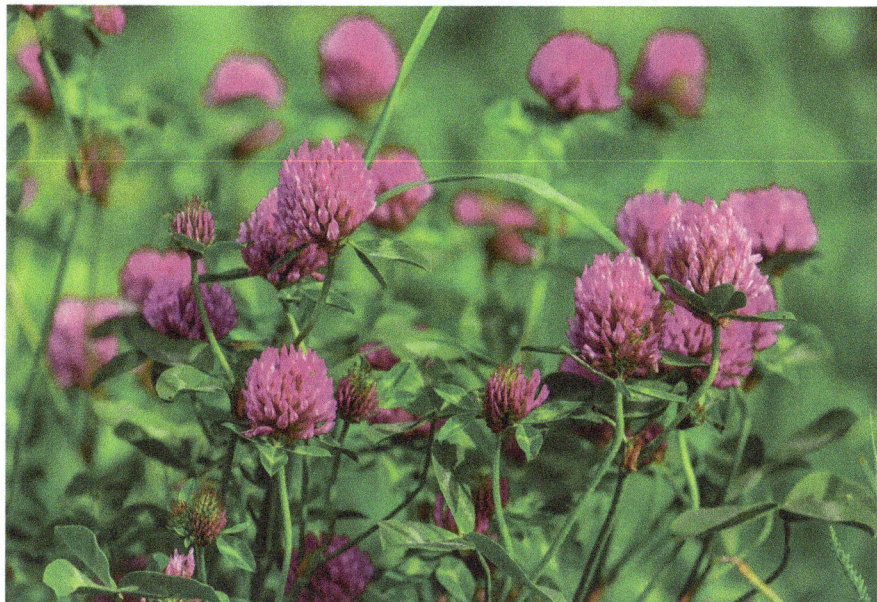

Red clover blossoms

and spreads its leaves above and its roots within the soil, keeping out weeds and protecting the land. In the spring it may be plowed under, and thus add again to the fertility. This is also an aesthetic crop, for a field of crimson clover in bloom is one of the most beautiful sights in our rural landscape.

Red clover has such deep florets that, of all our bees, only the bumblebees have sufficiently long tongues to reach the nectar. It is, therefore, dependent upon this bee for developing its seed, and the enlightened farmer of to-day looks upon the bumblebees as his best

Yellow or hop clover.   *Buffalo clover.*   *Rabbit-foot or pussy clover.*

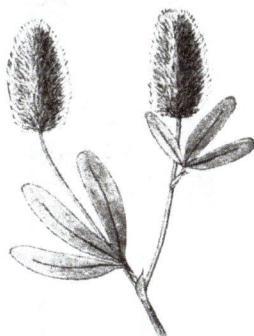

friends. The export of clover seed from the United States has sometimes reached the value of two million dollars per year, and this great industry can only be carried on with the aid of the bumblebee. There are sections of New York State where the growing of clover seed was once a most profitable business, but where now, owing to the dearth of bumblebees, no clover seed whatever is produced.

LESSON

Leading thought— The clovers enrich with nitrogen the soil in which they are planted. They are very valuable as food for stock; and their flowers are pollenated by bees.

Method— Each pupil should dig up a root of red clover or alfalfa to use for the lesson on the nodules. The flowers should be studied in the field, and also in detail in the schoolroom.

Observations—

1. How many kinds of clover do you know? How many of the medics?

2. In all clovers, which flowers of the head blossom first, those on the lower or outside, or those on the upper or inside?

3. Take up a root of red clover or alfalfa, noting how deep it grows. Wash the root free from soil, and find the little swellings on it. Write the story of what these swellings do for the clover, and incidentally for the soil.

4. How must the soil be prepared so that alfalfa may grow successfully? What does the farmer gain by feeding alfalfa, and why?

5. How do clover roots protect the land from being washed by heavy rains?

6. How do clovers keep the soil moist? How does this aid the farmer?

7. What is a cover crop, and what are its uses?

8. Upon what insects does the red clover depend for carrying pollen? Can it produce seed without the aid of these valuable bees? Why not?

Yellow sweet clover

Sweet Clover

TEACHER'S STORY

IN passing along the country roads, especially those which have suffered upheaval from the road machines, suddenly we are conscious of a perfume so sweet, so suggestive of honey and other delicate things, that we involuntarily stop to find its source. Close at hand we find this perfume laboratory in the blossoms of the sweet clover. It may be the species with white blossoms, or the one with yellow flowers, but the fragrance is the same. There stands the plant, lifting its beautiful blue-green foliage and its spikes of flowers for the enjoyment of the passer-by, while its roots are feeling their way down deep in the poor, hard soil, taking air and drainage with them and building, with the aid of their underground partners, nitrogen factories which will enrich the poverty-stricken earth, so that other plants may find nourishment in it.

Never was there such another beneficent weed as the sweet clover—beneficent alike to man, bee and soil. Usually we see it growing on soil so poor that it can only attain a height of from two to four feet; but if it once gets foothold on a generous soil, it rises majestically ten feet tall.

Like the true clover, its leaf has three leaflets, the middle one being longer and larger than the other two and separated from them by a naked midrib; the leaflets are long, oval in shape, with narrow, toothed edges, and they are dull, velvety green; the two stipules at the base of the leaf are little and pointed.

The blossoming of the sweet clover is a pretty story. The blossom stem, which comes from the axil of the leaf, is at first an inch or so long, packed closely with little, green buds having pointed tips. But as soon as the blossoming begins, the stem elongates, bringing the flowers farther apart—just as if the buds had been fastened to a rubber cord which had been stretched. The buds lower down open first; each day some of the flowers bloom, while those of the day before linger, and thus the blossom tide rises, little by little up the stalk. But the growing tip develops more and more buds, and thus the blossom story continues until long after the frosts have killed most other plants; finally the tip is white with blossoms, while the seeds developed from the first flowers on the plant have been perfected and scattered.

The blossom is very much like a diminutive sweet pea; the calyx is like a cup with five points to its rim, and is attached to the stalk by a short stem. The banner petal is larger than the wings and the keel. A lens shows the stamens united into two groups, with a thread-like pistil pushing out between; both stamens and pistil are covered by the keel, as in the pea blossom.

The flowers are beloved by bees and many other insects, which are attracted to them by their fragrance as well as by the white radiance of their blossoms. The ripened pod is well encased in the calyx at its base. The foliage of the sweet clover is fragrant, especially so when drying; it has been used for fodder. The sweet clovers came to us from Europe and are, in a measure, compensation for some of the other emigrant weeds which we wish had remained at home.

White sweet clover

LESSON

Leading thought— This beneficent plant grows in soil too poor for other plants to thrive in. It brings nitrogen and air into the soil, and thus makes it fertile so that other plants soon find in its vicinity nourishment for growth.

Method— Plants of the sweet clover with their roots may be brought to the schoolroom for study. The children should observe sweet clover in the field; its method of inflorescence, and the insects which visit it, should be noted.

Observations—

1. What first makes you aware that you are near sweet clover? On what kinds of soil, and in what localities, does sweet clover abound?

2. Do you know how sweet clover growing in poor soils and waste places acts as a pioneer for other plants?

3. Dig up a sweet clover plant, and see how far its stems go into the soil.

4. How high does the plant grow? What is the color of its foliage?

5. Compare one of the leaves with the leaf of a red clover, and describe the likeness and the difference. Note especially the edges of the upper and the lower leaves, and also the stipules.

Bee on some sweet clover

6. Describe the way the sweet clover blossoms. Do the lower or upper flowers open first? How does the flower stem look before it begins to blossom? What happens to it after the blossoming begins? How long will it continue to blossom?

7. Take a blossom and compare it with that of a sweet pea. Can you see the banner? The wings? The keel? Can you see if the stamens are united into two sets? Can you see the pistil? Note the shape of the calyx.

8. How many flowers are in blossom at a time? Does it make a mass of white to attract insects? In what other way does it attract insects? What insects do you find visiting it?

9. How do the ripened pods look?

"The blooming wilds His gardens are; some cheering
Earth's ugliest waste has felt that flowers bequeath,
And all the winds o'er summer hills careering
Sound softer for the sweetness that they breathe."

—THERON BROWN.

The White Clover

TEACHER'S STORY

THE sweet clover should be studied first, for after making this study it is easier to understand the blossoming of the white and the red clover. In the sweet clovers, the flowers are strung along the stalk but in the red, the white, and many others, it is as if the blossom stalk were telescoped, so that the flowers are all in one bunch, the tip of the stalk making the center of the clover head. We use the white clover in our lawns because of a peculiarity of its stem, which, instead of standing erect, lies flat on the ground, sending leaves and blossoms upward and thus making a thick carpet over the ground. The leaves are very pretty; and although they grow upon the stems alternately, they always manage to twist around so as to lift their three leaflets upward to the light. The three leaflets are nearly equal in size, with fine, even veins and toothed edges; and each has upon it, near the middle, a pale, angular spot. The white clover, in common with other clovers, has the pretty habit of going to sleep at night. Botanists may object to this human term, but the great Linnaeus first called it sleep, and we may be permitted to follow his example. Certainly the way the clover leaves fold at the middle, the three drawing near each other, looks like

going to sleep, and is one of the things which even the little child will enjoy observing.

The clover head is made up of many little flowers; each one has a tubular calyx with five delicate points and a little stem to hold it up into the world. In shape, the corolla is much like that of the sweet pea, and each secretes nectar at its base. The outside blossoms open first; and as soon as they are open, the honey bees, which eagerly visit white clover wherever it is growing, begin at once their work of gathering nectar and carrying pollen; as soon as the florets are pollenated they wither and droop below the flower-head.

"Where I made One, turn down an empty Glass."

Sings old Omar, and I always think of it when I see the turned-down florets of the white-clover blossom. But in this case the glass is not empty, but holds the maturing seed. This habit of the white clover flowers saves the bees much time, since only those which need pollenating are lifted upward to receive their visits. The length of time the little clover head requires for the maturing of its blossoms depends much upon the weather and upon the insect visitors.

White clover honey is in the opinion of many the most delicious honey made from any flowers except, perhaps, from orange blossoms. So valuable is the white clover as a honey plant, that apiarists often grow acres of it for their bees.

LESSON

Leading thought— The white clover has creeping stems. Its flowers depend upon the bees for their pollination, and the bees depend upon the white clover blossoms for honey.

Method— The plant may be brought into the schoolroom while in blossom, and its form be studied there. Observations as to the fertilization of the flowers should be made out-of-doors.

Observations—

1. Where does the white clover grow? Why is it so valuable in lawns?

2. Note carefully the clover leaf, the shape of the three leaflets, stems, and edges. Is part of the leaflet lighter colored than the rest? If so, describe the shape. Are the leaflets unequal or equal in size? Does each leaf come directly from the root? Are they alternately arranged? Why do they seem to come from the upper side of the stem?

3. Note the behavior of the clover leaves at night. How do the two side leaflets act? The central leaflet? Do you think that this is because the plant is sleepy?

4. Take a white clover head, and note that it is made up of many little flowers. How many? Study one of the little flowers with a lens. Can you see its calyx? Its petals? Its stem? In what way is it similar to the blossom of the sweet pea?

5. Take a head of white clover which has not yet blossomed. Tie a string about its stem so that you may be sure you are observing the

same flower and make the following observations during several days: Which blossoms begin to open first—those outside or inside? How many buds open each day? What happens to the blossoms as they fade? Of what use is this to the plant? How many days pass from the time the flowers begin to blossom until the last flower at the center opens?

6. What insects do you see working on the white clover blossoms? How does the bee act when collecting nectar? Can you see where she thrusts her tongue? What does the bee do for the clover blossom? What sort of honey does the white clover give to the bee?

7. Tie little bags of cheesecloth over two or three heads of white clover and see if they produce any seed.

> *"Little flower; but if I could understand*
> *What you are, root and all, and all in all,*
> *I should know what God and man is."*
>
> —TENNYSON.
>
> *"To me the meanest flower that blows, can give*
> *Thoughts that do often lie too deep for tears."*
>
> —WORDSWORTH.
>
> *"I know a place where the sun is like gold,*
> *And the cherry blooms burst with snow,*
> *And down underneath is the loveliest nook*
> *Where the four leaf clovers grow."*
>
> —ELLA HIGGINSON.

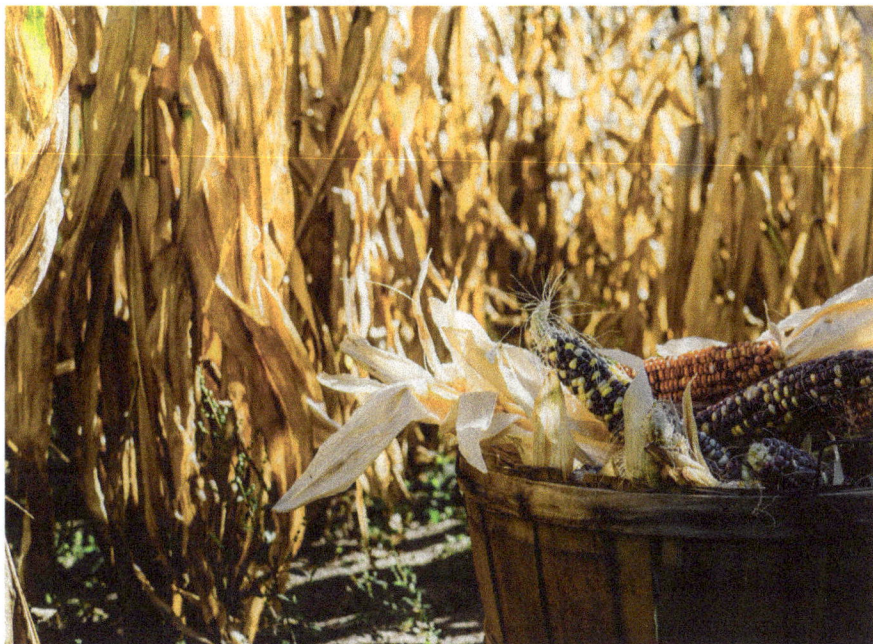

Various types of maize

The Maize, or Indian Corn

TEACHER'S STORY

"Hail! Ha-wen-ni-yu! Listen with open ears to the words of thy people. Continue to listen. We thank our mother earth which sustains us. We thank the winds which have banished disease. We thank He-no for rain. We thank the moon and stars which give us light when the sun has gone to rest. We thank the sun for warmth and light by day.

Keep us from evil ways that the sun may never hide his face from us for shame and leave us in darkness. We thank thee that thou hast made our corn to grow. Thou art our creator and our good ruler, thou canst do no evil. Everything thou doest is for our happiness."

THUS prayed the Iroquois Indians when the corn had ripened on the hills and valleys of New York State long before it was a state, and even before Columbus had turned his ambitious prows westward in quest of the Indies. Had he found the Indies with their wealth of fab-

195

rics and spices, he would have found there nothing so valuable to the world as has proved this golden treasure of ripened corn.

The origin of Indian corn, or maize, is shrouded in mystery. There is a plant which grows on the table-lands of Mexico, which is possibly the original species; but so long had maize been cultivated by the American Indians that it was thoroughly domesticated when America was first discovered. In those early days of American colonization, it is doubtful, says Professor John Fiske, if our forefathers could have remained here had it not been for Indian corn. No plowing, nor even clearing, was necessary for the successful raising of this grain. The trees were girdled, thus killing their tops to let in the sunlight, the rich earth was scratched a little with a primitive tool, and the seed put in and covered; and the plants that grew therefrom took care of themselves. If the pioneers had been obliged to depend alone upon the wheat and rye of Europe, which only grows under good tillage, they might have starved before they gained a foothold on our forest-covered shores.

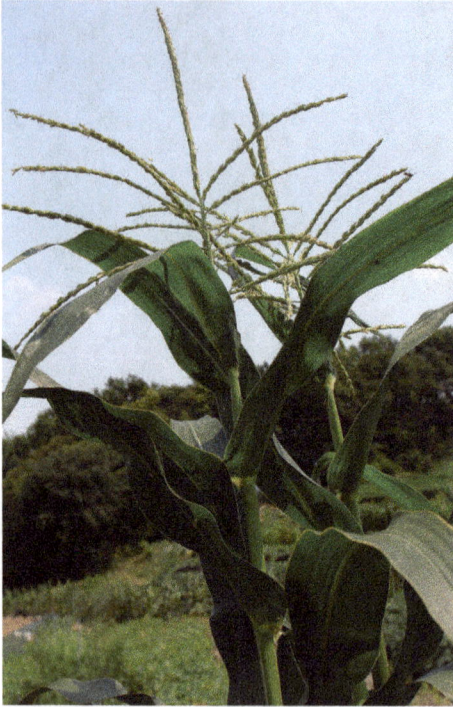

Corn tassels contain the bollen-bearing flowers

THE CORN PLANT

IN studying the maize it is well to keep in mind that a heavy wind is its worst enemy; such a wind will lay it low, and from such an injury it is difficult for the corn to recover and perfect its seed. Thus, the mechanism of the corn-stalk and leaf is adapted for prevention of this disaster. The corn-stalk is, practically, a strong cylinder with a pithy center; the fibres of the stalks are very strong, and at short intervals

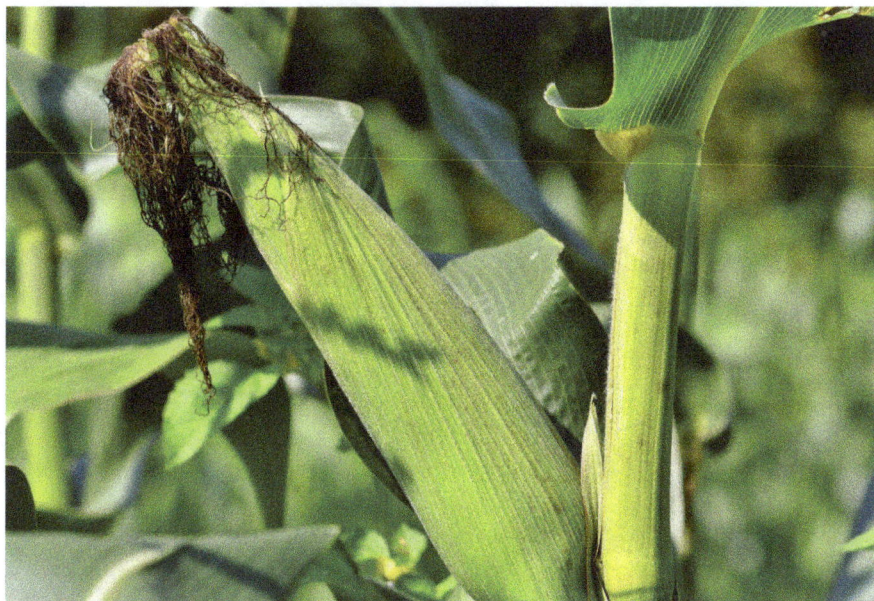

Corn leaves and a young cob

the stalk is strengthened by hard nodes, or joints.

If the whole stalk were as hard as the nodes, it would be inelastic and break instead of bend; as it is, the stalk is very elastic and will bend far over before it breaks. The nodes are nearer each other at the bottom, thus giving strength to the base; they are farther apart at the top, where the wind strikes, and where the bending and bowing of the stalk is necessary.

The leaf comes off at a node and clasps the stalk for a considerable distance, thus making it stronger, especially toward the base. Just where the leaf starts away from the stem there is a little growth called a rain-guard; if water should seep between the stalk and the clasping leaf, it would afford harbor for destructive fungi. The structure of the corn leaf is especially adapted to escape injury from the wind; the strong veins are parallel with a strong but flexible midrib at the center; often, after the wind has whipped the leaves severely, only the tips are split and injured. The edges of the corn leaf are ruffled and, where the leaf leaves the stalk, there is a wide fold in the edge at either side; this arrangement gives play for a sidewise movement without breaking the leaf margins. The leaf is thus protected from the wind, whether it is struck from above or horizontally. The true roots of the

A dried cob of corn

corn plant go quite deep into the soil, but are hardly adequate to the holding of such a tall, slender stalk upright in a wind storm; therefore, all about the base of the plant are brace-roots, which serve to hold the stalk erect—like the stay-ropes about a flagpole.

THE EAR OF CORN

THE ears of corn are borne at the joints or nodes; and the stalk, where the ear presses against it, is hollowed out so as to hold it snugly; this is very suggestive of a mother holding a baby in her arms. In the following ways, the husks show plainly that they are modified leaves: The husk has the same structure as the leaf, having parallel veins; it comes off the stem like a leaf; it is often green, and therefore does the work of a leaf; it changes to leaf shape at the tip of the ear, thus showing that the husk is really that part of the leaf which usually clasps the stem. If a husk tipped with a leaf is examined, the rain-guard will be found at the place where the two join. As a matter of fact, the ear of corn is on a branch stalk which has been very much shortened, so that the nodes are very close together, and therefore the leaves come off close together. By stripping the husks back one by one, the change from the outside, stiff, green leaf structure to the inner delicate, papery wrapping for the seed, may be seen in all its stages. This is a beautiful lesson in showing how the maize protects its seed, and the husk may well be compared to the clothing of a baby.

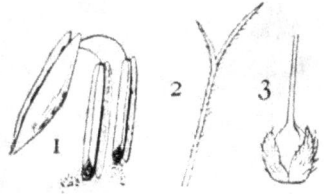

1. The anthers of corn. 2. The tip of the corn-silk showing the stigma. 3. The pistillate flower, which will develop into the kernel.

The pistillate flowers of the corn, which finally develop into the kernels, grow in pairs along the sides of the end portion of the shortened stalk, which is what we call the "cob." Therefore, the ear will show an even number of rows, and the cob shows distinctly that the rows are paired. The corn-silk is the style of the pistillate flowers; and therefore, in order to secure pollen, it must extend from the ovule, which later develops into a kernel, to the tip of the ear, where it protrudes from the end of the husk. A computation of the number of kernels in a row and on the ear makes a very good arithmetic lesson for the primary pupils, especially as the kernels occur in pairs.

THE GROWTH OF THE CORN

IF we cut a kernel of corn crosswise we can see, near the point where it joins the cob, the little plant and the root. Corn should be germinated between wet blotters, in a seed-testing experiment, before observations are made on the growing corn of the fields. When the corn first appears, the corn leaves are in a pointed roll which pierces the soil. Soon they spread apart, but it may be some time before the corn-stalk proper appears. Then it stretches up rapidly, and very soon will be tipped with beautiful pale brown tassels. These tassels merit careful study for they are the staminate flowers. Each floret has two anthers hanging down from it, and each half of each anther is a little bag of pollen-grains; and in order that they shall be shaken down upon the waiting corn-silk below, the bottom of each bag opens wide when the pollen is ripe. The corn-silk, at this stage, is branched at the tip and clothed with fine hairs, so that it may catch a grain of the precious pollen. Then occurs one of the most wonderful pollen stories in all nature, for the pollen-tube must push down through the center of

the corn-silk for its whole length, in order to reach the waiting ovule and thus enable it to become a kernel of corn. These young, unfertilized kernels are pretty objects, looking like seed-pearls, each wrapped in furry bracts. If the silk from one of these young flowers does not receive its grain of pollen, then the kernel will not develop and the ear will be imperfect. On the other hand if the pollen from another variety of corn falls upon the waiting stigmas of the silk, we shall find the ear will have upon it a mixture of the two varieties. This is best exemplified when we have the black and white varieties of sweet corn growing near each other.

One reason why corn is such a valuable plant to us is that its growth is so rapid. It is usually not planted until late spring, yet, with some varieties, by September the stalks are twenty feet high. The secret of this is that the corn, unlike many other plants, has many points of growth. While young, the lower part of the stalk lying between every two nodes is a growing center and the tip of the stalk also grows; in most plants, the tip of the stems is the only center of growth. The first two experiments suggested will demonstrate this. When blown down by the wind, the corn has a wonderful way of lifting itself, by inserting growing wedges in the lower sides of the nodes. A corn-stalk blown down by the wind will often show this wedge-shape at every joint, and the result will be an upward curve of the whole stalk. Of course, this cannot be seen unless the stalk is cut lengthwise through the center. Experiment 3 is suggested to demonstrate this.

During drought the corn leaves check the transpiration of water by rolling together lengthwise in tubes, thus offering less surface to the sun and air. The farmer calls this the curling of the corn, and it is always a sign of lack of moisture. If a corn plant with leaves thus curled, be given plenty of water, the leaves will soon straighten out again into their normal shape.

References: *Corn Plants*, Sargent; Cornell Nature-Study Leaflets, Vol. I; *Elements of Agriculture*, Warren; *The First Book of Farming*, Goodrich; *Agriculture*, Jackson and Dougherty; *Rural School Agriculture*, Hays; *Columbia's Emblem*, Houghton, Mifflin and Co.

LESSON

Leading thought— The Indian corn, or maize, is a plant of much beauty and dignity. It has wonderful adaptations for the development of its seed and for resisting its arch-enemy, the wind.

Method— The study may begin in spring when the corn is planted, giving the pupils the outline for observations to be filled out in their note-books during the summer, when they have opportunities for observing the plant; or it may be studied in the autumn as a matured plant. It may be studied in the school room or in the field, or both.

Observations on the corn plant—

1. Describe the central stem. How many joints, or nodes, has it? Of what use to the plant are these nodes? Are the joints nearer each other at the bottom or the top of the plant?

2. Where do the leaves come off the stem? Describe the relation of the bases of the leaves to the stem. Of what use is this to the plant?

3. Note the little growth on the leaf where it leaves the stalk. Describe how this prevents the rain from seeping down between the stalk and the clasping leaf. What danger would there be to the plant if the water could get into this narrow space?

4. What is the shape of the leaf? Describe the veins. Does the leaf tear easily across? Does it tear easily lengthwise? Of what use to the leaf is this condition?

Looking through corn rows

5. Are the edges of the corn leaf straight or ruffled? How does this ruffled edge permit the leaf to turn without breaking? Describe at length the benefit the corn plant derives from having leaves which cannot be broken across and that can bend readily sidewise as well as up and down.

6. Describe the roots of the corn plant. Describe the brace-roots. Explain their use.

7. Describe all the ways in which the corn plant is strengthened against its enemy, the wind.

Observations on the ear of corn—

8. Where on the corn plant are the ears borne? Are two ears borne on the same side of the stalk? Remove an ear, and see how the stalk is changed to give it room.

9. Where do the ears come off the stalk in relation to the leaves?

10. Examine the outside husks, and compare them with the green leaves. What is there to suggest that the corn-husk is a leaf changed to protect the seed? Do you think that the husk represents that portion of the leaf which clasps the stalk? Why? Describe how the inner husk differs from the outer in color and texture. Describe how this is a special protection to the growing kernels.

11. After carefully removing the husk, examine the silk and see if there is a thread for every kernel. Is there an equal amount of silk lying between every two rows? Do you know what part of the corn flower is the cornsilk? What part is the kernel?

12. How many rows of kernels are there on an ear? How many kernels in a row? How many on the whole ear? Do any of the rows disappear toward the tip of the ear? If so, do they disappear in pairs? Do you know why? Are the kernels on the tip of the ear and near the base as perfect as those along the middle? Do you know whether they will germinate as quickly and vigorously as the middle ones?

A corn shock. In regions where corn is not harvested by machinery, and where it is not used for silage, it is often shocked to permit it to mature

13. Study a cob with no corn on it and note if the rows of kernel-sockets are in distinct pairs. This will, perhaps, show best if you break the cob across.

14. Break an ear of corn in two, and sketch the broken end showing the relation of the cob to the kernels.

15. Are there any places on the ear you are studying, where the kernels did not grow or are blasted? What happened to cause this?

16. Describe the requisites for a perfect ear of seed-corn. Why should the plant from which the seed-ear is taken be vigorous and perfect?

Observations on the growth of corn—Work for the Summer Vacation—

17. How does the corn look when it first comes up? How many leaves are there in the pointed roll which first appears above the ground? How long before the central stalk appears?

Sugar cane, a near relative of corn, is a crop of tropical and subtropical regions. The stalks in the foreground have been stripped of leaves and are ready for the mill

18. When do the tassels first appear? What kind of flowers are the corn tassels? Describe the anthers. How many on each flower? Where do the anthers open to discharge their pollen?

19. How large are the ears when the pollen is being shed? Study an ear of corn at this period. Note that the kernel is the ovule, the silk is attached to it and is the long style extending out beyond the husks. Note that the tip, or stigma, is branched.

20. What carries the pollen for the corn plant? If you have rows of popcorn and sweet corn or of sweet corn and field corn next to each other, why is it that the ears will show a mixture of both kinds?

Experiment 1

Compare the growth of the corn plant with that of the pigweed. When the corn-stalk first appears above ground, tie two strings upon it, one just above a joint and one below it. Tie two strings the same distance apart on the stem of a pigweed. Measure carefully the distance between these two strings on the two plants. Two weeks later measure the distance between the strings again. What is the result?

Experiment 2

Measure the distance between two of the nodes or joints near the tip of a certain corn-stalk. Two weeks later measure this distance again and compare the two.

Experiment 3

When a stalk of corn is still green in August, bend it down and place a stick across it at about half its length. Describe how it tries to lift itself to an erect attitude after two or three weeks. Cut lengthwise across one of the nodes, beyond the point held down by the stick, and see the wedge-shaped growth within the joint which helps to raise the stalk to an upright position.

Experiment 4

During the August drought, note that the corn leaves are rolled. Give a corn plant with rolled leaves plenty of water and note what happens. Why?

Corn kernels

Cotton in a field

The Cotton Plant

TEACHER'S STORY

THERE are some plants which have made great chapters in the histories of nations, and cotton is one of them. The fibre of cotton was used for making clothing so long ago, that its discovery is shrouded in the myths of prehistoric times. But we believe it first came into use in India, for in this land we find certain laws concerning cotton which were codified 800 b.c.; and allusions to the fine, white raiment of the peoples of India are frequent in ancient history. Cotton was introduced into Egypt from India at an early date: it was in common use there 150 b.c. But not until our Civil War laid fallow the cotton fields of the United States, did Egypt realize the value of its crop; and although much money was lost there in agricultural speculation after our own product was again put on the market, yet cotton has remained since that time one of Egypt's most valuable exports.

When Columbus discovered America he found cotton growing in the West Indies, and the chief articles of clothing of the native Mexicans were made of cotton. Cloths of cotton were also found in ancient tombs of Peru, proving it was used there long before the white man set his foot upon those shores. When Magellan made his famous voyage around the world, beginning in 1519, he found the cotton fibre in use in Brazil.

It is a strange fact that the only region of the world between the parallels of 40° north and 40° south latitude, where cotton did not grow as a native or cultivated plant when America was discovered, was the region of our Gulf States, which now produces more cotton than any other. The first mention of cotton as a crop in the American colonies is in the report published in 1666. At the time of the Revolutionary War the cotton industry was thoroughly established. It is one of the significant facts of history that the invention of the cotton gin by Eli Whitney in 1793, which revolutionized the cotton industry and brought it to a much more profitable basis, wrought great evil to the United States, since it revived the profits of slave-holding. The institution of slavery was sinking out of sight by its own weight; Washington showed that it was the most expensive way to work land, and Jefferson failed to liberate his own slaves simply because he believed that liberty would come to all slaves inevitably, since slave-holding was such an expense to the plantation owners. But the cotton gin, which removed the seeds rapidly—theretofore done by slow and laborious hand process—suddenly made the raising of cotton so profitable that slaves were again employed in its production with great financial benefits. And thus it came about that the cotton plant innocently wielded a great influence in the political, as well as the industrial life of our country.

The cotton plant has a taproot, with branches which go deep into the soil. The stem is nearly cylindrical, the branches often spreading and sometimes irregular; the bark is dark and reddish; the wood is white. In Egypt, and probably in other arid countries, the stalks are gathered for fuel in winter.

The leaves are alternate, with long petioles. The upper leaves are deeply cut, some having five, some seven, some three, and some even nine lobes; strong veins extend from the petiole along the center of each lobe; the leaves near the ground may not be lobed at all. Where the petiole joins the stem, there is a pair of long, slender, pointed stipules,

Mature cotton bolls

but they often fall off early. A strange characteristic of the cotton leaves is that they bear nectar-glands; these may be seen on the under side and along the main ribs of the leaf; they appear as little pits in the rib; some leaves may have none, while others may have from one to five. It has been thought that perhaps these glands might attract bees, wasps or ants, which would attack the caterpillars eating the leaves, but this has not been proved. However, many friendly insects get their nectar at these leaf-wells, and here is an opportunity for some young naturalist of the South to investigate this matter and discover what insects come to these glands at all times of day and what they do.

The flower bud is partially hidden beneath the clasping bracts of the involucre. These bracts are three or four in number, and they have the edges so deeply lobed that they seem branched. By pushing back the bracts we can find the calyx, which is a shallow cup with five shallow notches in its rim. The petals are rolled in the bud like a shut umbrella. The open flower has five broadly spreading petals; when the bud first opens in the morning, the petals are whitish or pale yellow with a purplish spot at the base, by noon they are pale pink, by the next day they are a deep purplish red and they fall at the end of the second day. There are nectar-glands also in the flower at the base of the calyx, and the insects are obliged to thrust their tongues between the bases

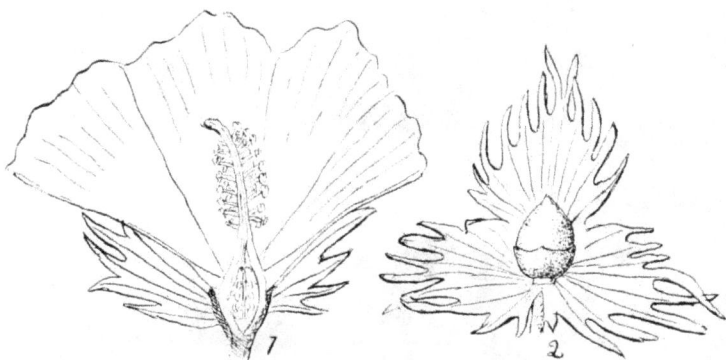

1. The cotton flower cut in half, showing the stamen-tube at the center, up through which extends the style of the pistil. Note the bracts and calyx.
2. A young boll, with calyx at its base and set in the involucral bracts.

of the petals to reach the nectar; only long-tongued bees, moths and butterflies are able to attain it.

There are many stamens which have their filaments united in a tube extending up into the middle of the flower and enlarging a little at the tip; below the enlarged base of this tube is the ovary which later develops into the cotton-boll; within the stamen-tube extends the long style, and from its tip are thrust out from three to five stigmas like little pennants from the top of a chimney; and sometimes they are more or less twisted together. The young boll is covered and protected by the fringed bracts, which cover the bud and remain attached to the ripened boll. The calyx, looking like a little saucer, also remains at the base of the boll. The boll soon assumes an elongated, oval shape, with long, pointed tip; it is green outside and covered with little pits, as large as pin points. There are, extending back from the pointed tip, three to five creases or sutures, which show where the boll will open. If we open a nearly ripened boll, we find that half way between each two sutures where the boll will open, there is a partition extending into the boll dividing it into compartments. These are really carpels, as in the core of an apple, and their leaf origin may be plainly seen in the venation. The seeds are fastened by their pointed ends along each side of the central edge of the partition, from which they break away very easily. The number of seeds varies, usually two or three along each side; the young seeds are wrapped in the young cotton, which is a stringy, soft white mass. The cotton fibres are attached to the covering

A cotton flower

of the seed around the blunt end, and usually the pointed end is bare. When the boll opens, the cotton becomes very fluffy and if not picked will blow away; for this cotton fibre is a device of the wild cotton for disseminating its seeds by sending them off on the wings of the wind. Heavy winds at the cotton-picking time, are a menace to the crop and often occasion serious loss.

The mechanism of the opening of the cotton-boll is very interesting; along the central edge of each partition and extending up like beaks into the point of the boll, is a stiff ridge, about the basal portion of which the seeds are attached; as the boll becomes dry, this ridged margin becomes as stiff as wire and warps outward; at the same time, the outside of the boll is shriveling. This action tears the boll apart along the sutures and exposes the seeds with their fluffy balloons to the action of the wind. The ripe, open, empty boll is worth looking at; the sections are wide apart and each white, delicate, parchment-like partition, or carpel, has its wire edge curved back gracefully. The outside of the boll is brown and shriveled, but inside it is still white and shows that it had a soft lining for its "seed babies."

The amount of the cotton crop per acre varies with the soil and climate; the amount that can be picked per day also depends upon the cotton as well as the picker. Children have been known to pick one hundred pounds per day, and a first-class picker from five hundred to six hundred pounds, or even eight hundred; one man has made a record of picking sixty pounds in an hour. Cotton is one of the most important crops grown in America, and there are listed more than one hundred and thirty varieties which have originated in our country.

References— The various bulletins of the United States Department of Agriculture and of the experiment stations of the Southern States. The most complete of these is Bulletin No. 33, Office of Experiment Stations, U. S. Dept. of Agriculture, published in 1896.

LESSON

Leading thought— Cotton has had a great influence upon our country politically as well as industrially. Its fibre was used by the ancients, and it is to-day one of the most important crops in the regions where it is grown.

Method— A cotton plant with blossoms and ripe bolls upon it may be brought into the school-room or studied in the field.

Observations—

1. How many varieties of cotton do you know? Which kind is it you are studying?

2. What sort of root has the cotton plant? Does it go deep into the soil?

3. How high does the plant grow? Are the stems tough or brittle? What is the color of the bark? Of the wood? Do you know of a country where cotton stalks are used for fuel? Do the stem and branches grow erect or very spreading?

4. Are the leaves opposite or alternate? Are the petioles as long as the leaves? Are there any stipules where the petioles join the main stem? How many forms of leaves can you find on the same stem? How do the upper differ from the lower leaves? Describe or sketch one of the large upper leaves, paying especial attention to the veins and the shape of the lobes.

5. Look at the lower side of a leaf and find, if you can, a little pit on the midrib near its base. How many of these pits can you find on the veins of one leaf? What is the fluid in these pits? Taste it and see if it is

sweet. Watch carefully a growing plant and describe what insects you find feeding on this nectar. Note if the wasps and ants, feeding on this nectar, attack the caterpillars of the cotton worm which destroy the leaf. Where are the nectar-glands of plants usually situated?

6. Study the flower bud; what covers it? How many of these bracts cover the flower bud? What is their shape and how do their edges look? Push back the bracts and find and describe the calyx. How are the petals folded in the bud?

7. Take the open flower; how many petals are there, and what is their shape? At what time of day do the flowers open? What color are the petals when the flowers first open? What is their color later in the day? What is their color the next day? When do the petals fall?

8. Describe the stamens; how are they joined? How are the anthers situated on the stamen-tube? Is the stamen-tube perfectly straight or does it bend at the tip?

9. Peel off carefully the stamen-tube and describe what you find within it. How many stigmas come out of the tip of the tube? Find the ovary below the stamen-tube. Which part of the flower grows into the cotton-boll?

10. Take a boll nearly ripe; what covers it? Push away the bracts;

can you find the calyx still present? What is the shape of the boll? What is its color and texture? Can you see the creases where it will open? How many are there of these?

Cotton bales on an old wagon

11. Open a nearly ripe boll very carefully. How many partitions are there in it? Where are they in relation to the openings? Gently push back the cotton from the seeds without loosening them, and describe how the seeds are connected with the partitions. Is the seed attached by its pointed or blunt end?

12. How many seeds in each chamber in the cotton boll? Where on the seed does the cotton grow? How does the cotton blanket wrap about the seed? If the cotton is not picked what happens to it? Of what use to the wild cotton plant are seeds covered with cotton?

13. What makes the cotton-boll open? Describe an open and empty boll outside and inside.

14. How much cotton is considered a good crop per acre in your vicinity? How much cotton can a good picker gather in a day?

15. Write English themes on the following topics: "The history of the cotton plant from ancient times until to-day," "How the cotton plant has affected American history."

> "Queen-consort of the kingly maize,
>   The fair white cotton shares his throne,
>   And o'er the Southland's realm she claims
>   A just allegiance, all her own."

—Minnie Curtis Wait.

A strawberry blossom

The Strawberry

TEACHER'S STORY

OF all the blossoms that clothe our open fields, one of the prettiest is that of the wild strawberry. And yet so influenced is man by his stomach that he seldom heeds this flower except as a promise of a crop of strawberries. It is comforting to know that the flowers of the field "do not care a rap" whether man notices them or not; insect attentions are what they covet, and they are surely as indifferent to our indifference as it is to them.

The field strawberry's five petals are little cups of white held up protectingly around a central treasure of anthers and pistils; each petal has its base narrowed into a little stem, which the botanists call a claw. When the blossom first opens, the anthers are little, flat, vividly lemon-yellow discs, each disc consisting of two clamped together sternly and determinedly as if they meant never to open and yield their gold dust. At the very center of the flower is a little, greenish yellow cone, which if we examine with a lens, we can see is made up of many pistils set together, each lifting up a little, circular, eager stigma high as ever it can reach. Whether all the stigmas receive pollen or not determines the formation of a good strawberry.

The sepals are slender and pointed and seem to be ten in number, every other one being smaller and shorter than its neighbors; but the

214

five shorter ones are not sepals but are bracts below the calyx. The sepals unite at their bases so that the strawberry has really a lobed calyx instead of separate sepals. The blossom stem is soft, pinkish and silky and wilts easily. There are several blossoms borne upon one stem and the central one opens first.

The strawberry leaf is beautiful; each of its three leaflets is oval, deeply toothed, and has strong regular veins extending from the midrib to the tip of each tooth. In color it is rich, dark green and turns to wine-color in autumn. It has a very pretty way of coming

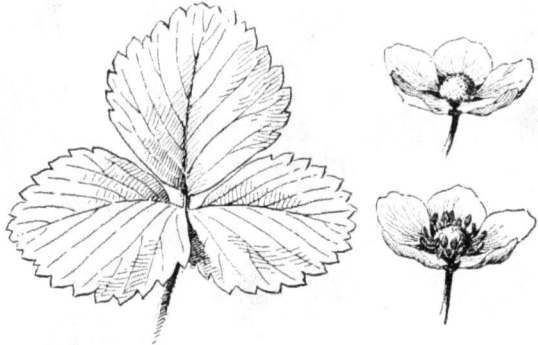

Left, a strawberry leaf. pistillate flower, right above. Perfect flower, right below.

out of its hairy bud scales, each leaflet folded lengthwise and the three pressed together. Its whole appearance then, is infantile in the extreme, it is so soft and helpless looking. But it soon opens out on its pink, downy stem and shows the world how beautiful a leaf can be.

If a comparison of the wild and cultivated strawberries is practicable, it makes this lesson more interesting. Much tillage and food have caused the cultivated blossoms to double, and they may often have seven or eight petals. And while the wild flowers are usually perfect, many cultivated varieties have the pollen and pistils borne in different flowers, and they depend upon the bees to carry their pollen. The blossom stem of the garden strawberry is round, smooth and quite strong, holding its branching panicle of flowers erect, and it is usually shorter than the leaf stems among which it nestles. The flowers open in a series, so that ripe and green fruit, flowers and buds may often be found on the same stem. As the strawberry ripens, the petals and stamens wither and fall away; the green calyx remains as the hull, which holds in its cup the pyramid of pistils which swell and ripen into the juicy fruit. To the botanists the strawberry is not a berry, that definition being limited to fruits having a juicy pulp and containing

The ripening process of a strawberry fruit. The unripe berry is white

many seeds, like the currant or grape. The strawberry is a fleshy fruit bearing its seed in shallow pits on its surface. These seeds are so small that we do not notice them when eating the fruit, but each one is a tiny nut, almond-shaped, and containing within its tough, little shell a starchy meat to sustain the future plant which may grow from it. It is by planting these seeds that growers obtain new varieties.

The root of the strawberry is fibrous and threadlike. When growers desire plants for setting new strawberry beds they are careful to take only such as have light colored and fresh-looking roots. On old plants the roots are rather black and woody and are not so vigorous.

The stem of the strawberry is partially underground and so short as to be unnoticeable. However, the leaves grow upon it alternately one above another, so that the crown rises as it grows. The base of each leaf has a broad, clasping sheath which partly encircles the plant and extends upward in a pair of earlike stipules.

The runners begin to grow after the fruiting season has closed; they originate from the upper part of the crown; they are strong, fibrous and hairy when young. Some are short between joints, others seem to reach far out as if seeking for the best location before striking root; a young plant will often have several leaves before putting forth roots. Each runner may start one or more new strawberry plants. After the young plant has root growth so as to be able to feed itself, the runner ceases to carry sap from the main stem and withers to a mere dry fiber. The parent plant continues to live and bear fruit, for the strawberry is a perennial, but the later crops are of less value. Gardeners usually renew their plots each year, but if intending to harvest a second year's crop, they cut off the runners as they form.

LESSON

Leading thought— The strawberry plant has two methods of perpetuating itself, one by the seeds which are grown on the outside of the strawberry fruits, and one by means of runners which start new plants wherever they find place to take root.

Method— It would be well to have a strawberry plant, with roots and runners attached, for an observation lesson by the class. Each pupil should have a leaf, including the clasping stipules and sheath at its base. Each one should also have a strawberry blossom and bud, and if possible a green or ripe fruit.

Observations—

1. What kind of root has the strawberry? What is its color?

2. How are the leaves of the strawberry plant arranged? Describe the base of the leaf and the way it is attached to the stem. Has each leaflet a pedicel or stem of its own? How many leaflets are there? Sketch a strawberry leaf, showing the edges and form of the leaflets, and the veins.

3. From what part of the plant do the runners spring? When do the runners begin to grow? Does the runner strike root before forming a new plant or does the little plant grow on the runner and draw sustenance from the parent plant?

4. What happens to the runners after the new plants have become established? Does the parent plant survive or die after it sends out many runners?

5. Describe the strawberry blossom. How many parts are there to the hull or calyx? Can you see that five of these are set below the other five?

The wild strawberry looks very different to its cultivated cousins

6. How many petals has it? Does the number differ in different flowers? Has the wild strawberry as many petals as the cultivated ones?

7. Study with a lens the small green button at the center of the flower. This is made up of pistils so closely set that only their stigmas may be seen. Do you find this button of pistils in the same blossom with the stamens? Does the wild blossom have both stamens and pistils in the same flower?

8. Describe the stamens. What insects carry pollen for the strawberry plants?

9. Are the blossoms arranged in clusters? Do the flowers all open at the same time? What parts of the blossom fall away and what parts remain when the fruit begins to form?

10. Are the fruits all of the same shape and color? Is the pulp of the same color within as on the surface? Has the fruit an outer coat or skin? What are the specks on its surface?

11. How many kinds of wild strawberries do you know? How many kinds of cultivated strawberries do you know?

12. Describe how you should prepare, plant and care for a strawberry bed.

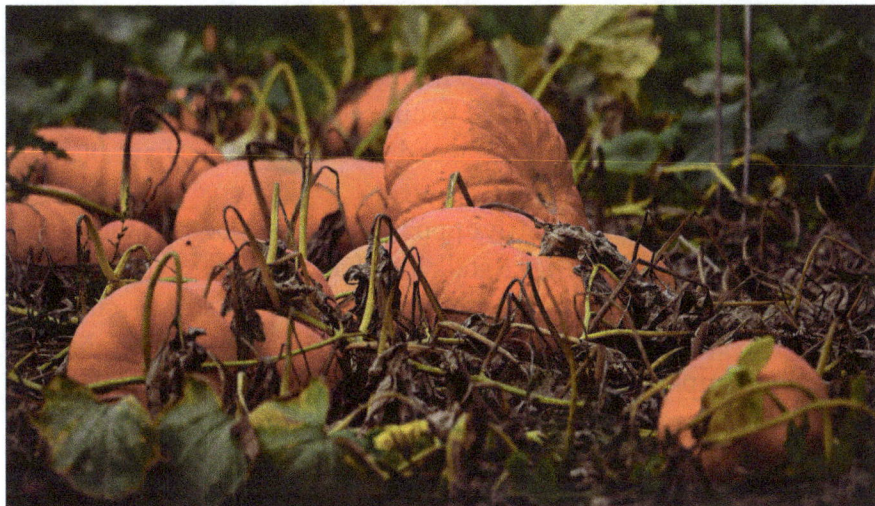

Pumpkins in a field

The Pumpkin

TEACHER'S STORY

IF the pumpkin were as rare as some orchids, people would make long pilgrimages to look upon so magnificent a plant. Although it trails along the ground, letting Mother Earth help it support its gigantic fruit, yet there is no sign of weakness in its appearance; the vine stem is strong, ridged, spiny and purposeful. And the spines upon it are surely a protection under some circumstances, for I remember distinctly when, as children, bare-footed and owning the world, we "played Indian" and found our ambush in the long rows of ripening corn, we skipped over the pumpkin vines, knowing well the punishment they inflicted on the unwary feet.

From the hollow, strongly angled stem arise in majesty the pumpkin leaves, of variously lobed patterns, but all formed on the same decorative plan. The pumpkin leaf is as worthy of the sculptor's chisel as is that of the classic *acanthus;* it is palmately veined, having from three to five lobes, and its broad base is supported for a distance on each side of the angled petiole by the two basal veins. The leaves are deep green above, paler below and are covered on both sides with minute bristles, and their edges are finely toothed. The bristly, angled stem

219

which lifts it aloft is a quite worthy support for so beautiful a leaf. And, during our childhood, it was also highly esteemed as a trombone, for it added great richness of quality to our orchestral performances, balancing the shrillness of the basswood whistle and the sharp buzzing of the dandelion-stem pipe.

Growing from a point nearly opposite a leaf, may be seen the pumpkin's elaborate tendril. It has a stalk like that of the leaf, but instead of the leaf blade it seems to have the three to five naked ribs curled in long, small coils very even and exact. Perhaps, at some period in the past, the pumpkin vines lifted themselves by clinging to trees, as do the gourd vines of to-day. But the pumpkin was cultivated in fields with the maize by the North American Indians, long before the Pilgrim Fathers came to America, to make its fruit into pies. Since the pumpkin cannot sustain itself in our Northern climate without the help of man, it was evidently a native of a warmer land; and, by growing for so long a time as a companion of the corn, it has learned to send its long stems out for many feet, resting entirely upon the ground. But, like a conservative, elderly maiden lady, it still wears corkscrew curls in memory of a fashion, long since obsolete. Occasionally, we see the pumpkin vines at the edge of the field pushing out and clambering over stone piles, and often attempting to climb the rail fences, as if there still remained within them the old instinct to climb.

But though its foliage is beautiful, the glory of the pumpkin is its vivid yellow blossom and, later, its orange fruit. When the blossom first starts on its career as a bud, it is enfolded in a bristly, ribbed calyx with five stiff, narrow lobes, which close up protectingly about the green, cone-shaped bud, a rib of the cone appearing between each two lobes of the calyx. If we watch one of these buds day after day, we find that the green cone changes to a yellow color and a softer texture as the bud unfolds, and then we discover that it is the corolla itself; however, these ribs which extend out to the tip of the corolla-lobes remain greenish below, permanently. The expanding of the flower bud is a pretty process; each lobe, supported by a strong midrib, spreads out into a five-pointed star, each point being very sharp and angular because, folded in along these edges in one of the prettiest of Nature's hems, is the ruffled margin of the flower. Not until the sun has shone upon the star for some little time of a summer morning, do these turned-in margins open out; and, late in the afternoon or during a storm, they fold down again neatly before the lobes close up; if a bee is not lively in escaping she may, willy-nilly, get a night's lodging, for these folded edges literally hem her in.

The story of the treasure at the heart of this starry, bell-shaped flower is a double one, and we

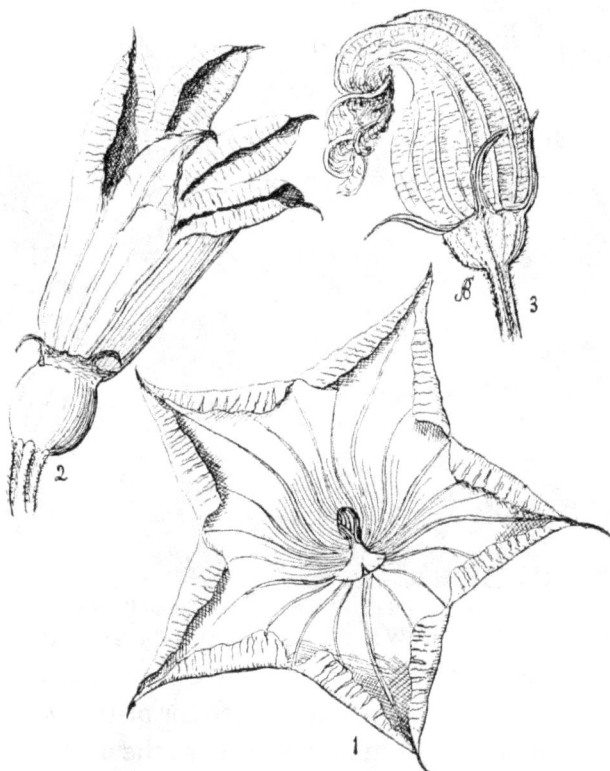

The closing of a pumpkin flower.
1. Staminate flower beginning to close; note the folded edges of the lobes. 2. Pistillate flower nearly closed. 3. Staminate flower closed and in its last stage.

had best begin it by selecting a flower that has below it a little green globe—the ovary—which will later develop into a pumpkin. At the heart of such a flower there stand three stigmas, that look like liliputian boxing-gloves; each is set on a stout, postlike style, which has its base in a great nectar-cup, the edges of which are slightly incurved over its welling sweetness. In order to reach this nectar, the lady bee must stand on her head and brush her pollen-dusted side against the greedy stigmas. Professor Duggar has noted that in dry weather the margins of this nectar-cup contract noticeably, and that in wet weather the stigmas close down as if the boxing-gloves were on closed fists.

The other half of the pumpkin-blossom story is to be found in the flowers which have no green globes below them, for these produce the

The staminate blossom of the pumpkin showing the anther knob

pollen. Such a flower has at its center a graceful pedestal with a broad base and a slender stem, which upholds a curiously folded, elongate knob, that looks like some ancient or primitive jewel wrought in gold. The corrugations on its surface are the anther-cells, which are curiously joined and curved around a central oblong support; by cutting one across, we can see plainly the central core, bordered by cells filled with pollen. But where is the nectar well in the smooth cup of this flower? Some have maintained that the bees visit this flower for the sake of the pollen, but I am convinced that this is not all of the story. In the base of the pedestal which supports the anther knob there appear, after a time, three inconspicuous openings; and if we watch a bee, we shall see that she knows these openings are there and eagerly thrusts her tongue down through them. If we remove the anthers and the pedestal, we shall find below the latter, a treasure cave; it is carpeted with the softest of buff velvet, and while it does not reek with nectar, as does the cup which encompasses the styles of the pistil, yet it secretes enough of the sweet fluid so that we can taste it distinctly. Thus, although the bees find pollen in this flower they also find there, nectar. The pumpkin is absolutely dependent upon the work of bees and other insects for carrying its pollen from the blossom that bears it to the one

222

which needs it, as this is the only way that the fruit may be developed.

And after the pollen has been shed and delivered, the flower closes, this time with an air of finality. The fading corolla looks as if its lobes had been twisted about by the thumb

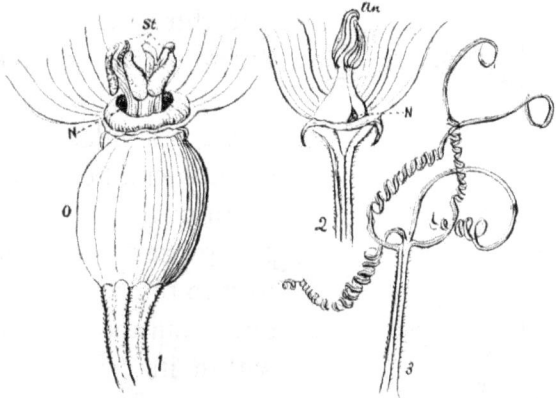

1. Base of pistillate blossom; O, ovary which develops into the pumpkin; n, nectar cup; st., stigmas. 2. Base of a staminate blossom; n, opening into the nectar cup; an, anthers joined, forming a knob. 3. Pumpkin tendril.

and finger to secure tightness; and woe betide the bee caught in one of these prisons, unless she knows how to cut through its walls or can find within, sustenance to last until the withered flower falls. The young pumpkin is at first held up by its stiff stem but later rests upon the ground.

The ripe pumpkin is not only a colossal but also a beautiful fruit. The glossy rind is brilliant orange and makes a very efficient protection for the treasures within it. The stem is strong, five-angled and stubborn, and will not let go its hold until the fruit is over-ripe. It then leaves a star-shaped scar to match the one at the other end of the fruit, where once the blossom sat enthroned. The pumpkin in shape is like a little world flattened at the poles, and with the lines of longitude creased into its surface. But the number of these longitudinal creases varies with individual pumpkins, and seems to have no relation to the angles of the stem or the three chambers within.

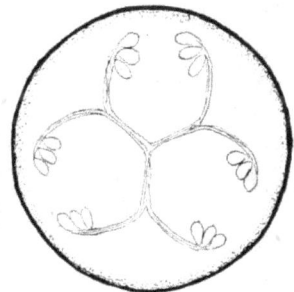

If we cut a small green pumpkin across, we find the entire inside solid. There are three fibrous partitions extending from the center, dividing the pulp

Section of a pumpkin just after the blossom has fallen. Note how the seeds are borne.

The squash plant breaking out of the seed-coats.

The operation further progressed.

into thirds; at its outer end each partition divides, and the two ends curve in opposite directions. Within these curves the seeds are borne. A similar arrangement is seen in the sliced cucumber. As the pumpkin ripens, the partitions surrounding the seeds become stringy and very different from the "meat" next to the rind, which makes a thick, solid outer wall about the central chamber, where, within its "groined arches" are contained six rows of crowded seeds, attached by their pointed tips and supported by a network of yellow, coarse fibers—like babies supported in hammocks. All this network, making a loose and fibrous core, allows the seeds to fall out in a mass when the pumpkin is broken. If we observe where the cattle have been eating pumpkins we find these masses of seeds left and trampled into the mud, where, if our winter climate permitted, they could grow into plants next year.

The pumpkin seed is attached by its pointed end; it is flat, oblong and has a rounded ridge at its edge, within which is a delicate "beading." The outside is very mucilaginous; but when wiped dry, we can see that it has an outer, very thin, transparent coat; a thicker white, middle coat; while the meat of the seed is covered with a greenish, membranous coat. The meat falls apart lengthwise and flatwise, the two halves forming later the seed-leaves and containing the food laid up by the "pumpkin mother" for the nourishment of the young plant. Between these two halves, at the pointed end, is the germ, which will develop into a new plant.

A pumpkin vine will use its tendrils grow over almost any structure

When sprouting, the root pushes out through the pointed end of the seed and grows downward. The shell of the seed is forced open by a little wedge-shaped projection, while the seed-leaves are pulled from their snug quarters. In watching one of these seeds sprout, it is difficult not to attribute to it conscious effort, while it is sturdily pulling hard to release its seed-leaves. If it fails to do this, the seed shell clamps the seed-leaves together like a vise, and the little plant is crippled.

Both squashes and pumpkins figure in the spicy Thanksgiving pies, but the chief value of the pumpkin crop in America is as food for milch cows; it causes a yield of milk so rich, that the butter made from it is as golden as its flesh. But the Hallow-e'en jack o'lantern appeals to the children. In this connection, a study of expression might be made interesting; the turning of the corners of the mouth up or down, and the angles of the eyebrows, making all the difference between a jolly grin and an "awful face."

LESSON

Leading thought— The pumpkin and squash were cultivated by the American Indians in their cornfields long before Columbus discovered the new world. The flowers of these plants depend entirely upon

Pumpkins and squash come in many varieties

insects for carrying their pollen, and are unable to develop their fruit without this aid.

Method— This work may be done in the garden or field in September or early October; or a vine bearing both kinds of flowers, leaves and tendrils may be brought to the schoolroom for observation. The lesson on the pumpkin fruit may be given later. A small green pumpkin should be studied with the ripe one, and also with the blossoms, so as to show the position of the seeds during development. This lesson can be modified to fit the cucumber, the melon and the squash.

THE PUMPKIN VINE AND FLOWERS

Observations—

1. How many different forms of flowers do you find on a pumpkin vine? What are the chief differences in their shape?

2. Look first at the flowers with the long slender stems. What is the shape and color of the blossom? How many lobes has it? Is each lobe distinctly ribbed or veined? Is the flower smooth on the inner and the outer surface? Are the edges of the lobes scalloped or ruffled?

3. What do you see at the bottom of the golden vase of this flower?

This yellow club, or knob, is formed by the joining of three anthers, one of which is smaller than the others. Do all the pumpkin flowers have this knob at the center? Look at the base of the standard which bears the anther-knob, and note if there are some openings; how many? Cut off the anther pedestal, and describe what is hidden beneath it. Note if the bees find the openings to the nectar-well and probe there for the nectar. Do they become dusted with pollen while seeking the nectar?

4. What color is the pollen which is clinging to the anther? Is it soft and light, or moist and sticky? Do you think that the wind would be able to lift it from its deep cup and carry it to the cup of another flower?

5. Describe the calyx behind this pollen-bearing flower. How many lobes has it? Are the lobes slender and pointed?

6. Find one of the flowers which has below it a little green globe, which will later develop into a pumpkin. How does this flower differ from the one that bears the pollen?

7. Describe or sketch the pistil which is at the bottom of this flower vase. Into how many lobes does it divide? Do these three stigmas face outward, or toward each other? Are the styles which uphold the stigmas short or long? Describe the cup in which they stand. Break away a bit of this little yellow cup and taste it. Why do you think the pumpkin flowers need such a large and well-filled nectary? Could insects get the nectar from the cup without rubbing against the stigmas, the pollen with which they became so thoroughly dusted when they visited the staminate flowers?

8. Cut through the center of one of the small green pumpkins. Can you see into how many sections it is divided? Does the number of seed-clusters correspond with the number of stigmas in the flower? Make a sketch of a cross-section, showing where the seeds are placed.

9. What insects do you find visiting the pumpkin flowers?

10. Carefully unfold a flower bud which is nearly ready to open, and note how it is folded. Then notice late in the afternoon how the flower closes. What part is folded over first? What next? How does it look when closed?

11. Describe the stems of the pumpkin vine; how are they strengthened and protected? Sketch or describe a pumpkin leaf.

12. Describe one of the tendrils of the pumpkin vine. Do you think that these tendrils could help the vine in climbing? Have you ever found a pumpkin vine climbing up any object?

THE PUMPKIN FRUIT

Observations—

1. Do you think the pumpkin is a beautiful fruit? Why? Describe its shape and the way it is creased. Describe the rind, its color and its texture, and tell how it protects the fruit. Describe the stem; does it cling to the pumpkin? How many ridges in the stem where it joins the vine? How many where it joins the pumpkin? Which part of the stem is larger? Does this give it a firmer hold?

2. Cut in halves crosswise a small green pumpkin and a ripe one. Which is the most solid? Can you see how the seeds are borne in the green pumpkin? How do they look in the ripe pumpkin? What is next to the rind in the ripe fruit? What part of the pumpkin do we use for pies?

3. Can you see in the ripe pumpkin where the seeds are borne? How are they suspended? How many rows of seeds length-wise of the pumpkin? Of what use could it be to the pumpkin to have the seeds thus suspended within it by these threads or fibers? What is left of a pumpkin after the cattle have eaten it? Might the seeds thus left plant themselves?

4. Is the pumpkin seed attached at the round, or the pointed, end? Describe the pumpkin seed, its shape and its edges. How does it feel when first taken from the pumpkin? How many coats has the seed?

5. Describe the meat of the seed. Does it divide naturally into two parts? Can you see the little germ? Have you ever tried roasting and salting pumpkin and squash seeds, to prepare them for food as almonds and peanuts are prepared?

6. Plant a pumpkin seed in damp sand and give it warmth and light. From which end does it sprout? What comes first, the root or the leaves? What part of the seed forms the seed-leaves?

7. Describe how the pumpkin sprout pries open the shell to its seed, in order to get its seed-leaves out. What happens if it does not

pull them out? Which part of the seedling pumpkin appears above ground first?

8. How do the true leaves differ in shape from the seed-leaves? What is the use of the seed-leaves to the plant?

> Ah! on Thanksgiving day, when from East and from West,
> From North and from South come the pilgrim and guest,
> When the gray-haired New-Englander sees round his board
> The old broken lines of affection restored,
> When the care-wearied man seeks his mother once more,
> And the worn matron smiles where the girl smiled before,
> What moistens the lip and brightens the eye?
> What calls back the past, like the rich Pumpkin pie?
> Oh, fruit loved of boyhood! the old days recalling,
> When wood-grapes were purpling and brown nuts were falling
> When wild, ugly faces we carved in its skin,
> Glaring out through the dark with a candle within!
> When we laughed round the corn-heap, with hearts all in tune,
> Our chair a broad pumpkin—our lantern the moon,
> Telling tales of the fairy who travelled like steam,
> In a pumpkin-shell coach, with two rats for her team!
>
> —J. G. WHITTIER.